What's the Story?

What story are you telling yourself
about your body and its existence?

By Nia Patterson

What's the Story?
Nia Patterson

First Published in the USA in 2023 by Nia Patterson LLC

hello@niapatterson.com

Book Editor: Cori Rupe
Book Cover: Nia Patterson

ISBN: 979-8-9894321-0-3 (Paperback)
ISBN: 979-8-9894321-3-4 (eBook)

www.niapatterson.com

First edition 2023

DISCLAIMER: This journal is a self-paced self-reflection tool. I do not consider it a substitute or equivalent to therapy. This is much more akin to body image coaching practices. If you are facing emotional or psychological struggles more akin to therapy practices, please consult a licensed therapist or mental health professional.

To Amee.

Who taught me that food is more than nourishment. It is, in fact, satiation, satisfaction, and sensation. It is home. And that I was allowed to find a home within it.

And you, dear reader, are allowed to, too.

This QR Code links to a website that contains access to all of the links and resources mentioned in this book. You can also find direct links at the back of the book.

https://www.niapatterson.com/what-s-the-story-links

Table of Contents

Introduction

Hello Friend, and welcome to *What's the Story?*

Are you sitting outside your therapist's office cracking this book open? Are you sitting on the toilet in a silent moment of solitude at work, seeking respite from your brain's torrential downpour of rudeness against you? Are you sitting outside the dressing room while your friend tries on the latest pink Barbie outfit in Forever 21?

Honestly, that last one was me in 2012. I was sitting outside the changing room in Forever 21 while my much thinner (straight-sized in clothes) friend tried on clothes I could only dream of trying on—don't worry, the Barbie movie wasn't a thing yet. And I was watching Grey's Anatomy for the very first time on my iPhone. I was literally sitting in Forever 21 on a white sofa, crying about some fictional person being stuck in a sinkhole, while my friend was oblivious to how much those tears weren't just about that person in the sink hole. They were also about how my body felt like an abomination in rags—I didn't fit into anything in that store.

What I'm saying is that wherever you're calling in from—reading in from—chances are you're not the only one. You are not alone here.

I didn't set out to make this book. No, in fact, months ago, I was in a pit deeper and darker than one I'd been in for a long time, and I needed money. I *needed* money. As in, I gave my last hundreds of dollars away and was hemorrhaging. I was paying bills with money I didn't have, and I thought to myself, wow, what can I help others with? What path can I walk them along that I know well enough to teach someone something about?

It dawned on me that it might be body liberation or recovery or getting out from under a world of diet culture. I felt like that might be all I was good for— talking about how to love your body when the world around you wants so desperately for you to HATE it.

And so, I worked for months. I developed a coaching program built on the back of my own journey from self-loathing to I-kinda-like-myself-but-also-on-bad-days-it's-still-hard-ville. Ya been there? She's rad.

Oh, wait. I've gotten this far in, and I haven't told you who I am. Shit. Shit. Shit. Okay. Okay. Let's do this.

I'm Nia Patterson. I use the pronouns they/them. I identify as the Queer, Trans, Nonbinary Black Auntie who probably needed growing up but didn't get. And if you did get a super cool Queer, Black Auntie growing up, then your Auntie is probably the Auntie I didn't get.

So, here's the thing. I hate, abhor, introducing myself. It's the hardest thing for me to do. I'm funny as shit sometimes, but I just suck at introducing myself. And the best part is that every time I introduce myself, it always changes based on what is top-of-mind at the time. You never know what you're going to get with this one.

Alright. I'm 31 (at the time of writing this). I'm an Autistic ADHDer who lives with cPTSD, PTSD, anxiety, and OCD—and is in pretty rockin' recovery from an eating disorder. I am 5'2 and ¾ inches tall. I won't tell you what I weigh, but let's just say if you saw me in person, you might be surprised that I am THAT FAT. Yes, I am fatter in real life than you may have thought, and that's actually kinda cool. I have short black hair and am rocking it. I nearly always have ashy ankles and ashy knees—sorry, Gram! My arms have tattoos along them. And I have a dangerously gorgeous FUPA that hangs over my waistband—if you didn't know, that stands for Fat, Upper, Pussy, Area. Yea.

A fun fact about me is that I hate grammar rules and writing how I'm "supposed to," so you may see some weird sentences here and there, or the sentence structure may be off from "proper English", but I'll tell you what, it's on par for how I talk in real life. So, if you've got an inner dialogue, then you're probably accidentally listening to me in your head. And if you don't have an inner dialogue... well... how's life treating you?

Anyway, I digress. Where was I?

Ah. Money. Yea. That.

I set out with the intention of launching my first coaching business, making a ton of money, bathing in dollar bills, and living the good life. But none of that happened. You know why? Even though my heart was in the exact right place, it was also too hard to find. What do I mean by that? What I mean is that even though I wanted to help people and desperately wanted to cure eating disorders, diet culture, and more, I was exhausted, I was burnt out, and so, so, so unhappy. I was trying to capitalize on my own knowledge, but I was also trying to do what I knew I truly wanted to do.

Writing these pages to release this book is the first time in weeks I have felt jazzed enough about something to take my computer to bed and stay up past my bedtime.

So, all this to say that I am relinquishing these words to your hands. I have spiffed them up enough to be in book format, but really, they're for you. They're for you to read and learn and soak up and apply. Because if there's one thing I want, it's for people like you—like 2012 Nia outside that dressing room—to know the truth. The truth about how I fought back against my own fatphobia, my own anti-fat bias, and my own inherent hatred of myself. I want you to know the steps I took to get here and the tools I figured out along the way to reach I-kinda-like-myself-but-also-on-bad-days-it's-still-hard-ville so that you can apply them yourself and, hopefully, join me here one day.

I won't lie to you. It takes time, gaining weight (for most of us), gaining insight (for all of us), and tackling our internalized bullshit head-on every day, but you've got this. I know you do. If you're anything like me, you'll make it through tough and easy and the shitstorm in between.

Sending you love, body liberation warrior.

You got this.

Nia

Part 1

Getting Comfortable Being Uncomfortable

A NOTE BEFORE YOU HOP IN...

Some of this part (and this first step, in particular) WILL be uncomfy or hard, challenging or difficult. That is expected and okay. That is part of why we are here doing this work. If you're feeling uncomfortable or unable to move forward in this work, please, PLEASE reach out to me via email or DMs, and we will schedule a time (free of cost) so that you feel heard, taken seriously, cared for, and so that you can better move forward if you choose to.

(🔗 Remember to use the QR code at the beginning or find the links at the back of the book when going through.)

"I Commit" Statement

This is completely up to you, but something I ask the clients I've worked with to do is to commit to certain guidelines or strong suggestions while they engage directly with the work we're taking on. This commitment is to not only do things like feed your brain and your needs but also to give you the best chance of understanding and implementing the content in this book. So, feel free to cross out any of the statements below and, maybe, even add a few of your own below.

While Reading this Book, I Commit to...

* Not weighing myself
* Trying MY best to implement what I learn in this book (this doesn't mean I need to do it perfectly or anyone else's way—it is truly MY best)
* Making time during the day to do SOME work on something in this book/journal
* Not actively engaging in intentional weight loss
* Not prioritizing weight loss over my physical or mental health
* Not berating myself for doing anything in this book "wrong"
  (Note: There is no "wrong" here)

Introduction to Body Image + Body Liberation

Introduction: _In this section, you should expect to learn about the basics of what I consider the definitions of body image, body liberation, body neutrality, and body positivity to be. I realize this is specific to me and could be different from how others define these things. And I want to let you know that that's perfectly fine. At each point in this book, feel free to_ **chew the meat and spit out the bones**_—keep what resonates, and let the rest go._

Here, we will dive into the history of these terms where necessary and how they show up in today's world—and also how they might apply to you, in particular.

🫘 _Keep in Mind:_ **You can answer the upcoming questions (really, all questions you'll find in this book) in whatever way feels good to you. On a scale of 1-5, a Yes or No, a lengthy paragraph, colors, drawings, or whatever else you come up with! Your journal and how you choose to answer the questions are solely up to you. Do not let your brain dictate that there is a "right" or "wrong" way because I promise you <u>there is not</u>.**

Questions to Answer First

What is your current knowledge of weight stigma, body liberation, body positivity, and body-based oppression? How would you define these terms?

In what ways have you directly experienced or been affected by body-based oppression in your lifetime? Please take into consideration body size/weight as well as race, gender, neurodivergence, disability, sexual orientation, and/or whatever else you feel is pertinent for you.

In what ways have you perpetuated body-based oppression against others?

What are your personal observations of how we [the people in the world around you] talk about bodies, in general and specifically?

What are your personal observations of how you yourself talk about bodies in the world around you?

How has the body-based oppression you have experienced in the world been detrimental or beneficial to you? This can be in regard to your mental health, disordered eating (or an eating disorder), medical care, body image, consistent dieting, workplace discrimination, and wherever else you feel you've been affected.

Defining Body-Based Terminology

I want you to realize that everyone in this community has different ways of defining various body liberation terms. I have been around awhile, but still, those before me in this space may define these in their own way, and I know for sure that many people who came to this space after me define these terms differently than me as well. But when I give speeches and talks, this is how I define them...

First up is body image. I think of body image as the various ways in which we, ourselves, perceive our own bodies. This can mean that we are feeling in alignment with positive views about our bodies on a given day, or we can feel out of alignment and confused, or even negatively toward our bodies. If we perceive our body as "too big", "too ugly", or "not pretty" enough, these thoughts directly affect our perceptions and beliefs about our bodies at that moment.

Second up is body liberation. I define body liberation as a socio-political justice movement for the freedom and liberation of marginalized bodies from a system of body-based oppression that delineates people in bodies that are not "the norm" as unworthy, unhealthy, less than, or not desirable. This may sound simple and unaffecting in text. Still, when systems of oppression lead to not hiring fat people, firing disabled people, and attacking transgender, two-spirit, non-binary, or gender expansive folx, then the system is not built to keep marginalized folx safe. It's built to tear them to pieces. One of the most intense, and far too common, outcomes of a system built on the oppression of different bodies is death---this is not even considered uncommon.

We cannot define body liberation without defining body-based oppression and weight stigma. Most simply put, "Body-based oppression is about how the world around us treats our bodies."[1] Some common identities that are historically discriminated against through body-based oppression are race, gender, and ability. And a not-as-well-known identity that is often discriminated against is weight/body size (but you know this now because you're reading this book!).

Weight stigma is this more specific form of body-based oppression that is focused on the body size and/or weight of a person and the perceived meaning of a person being fat (i.e., assuming that person is lazy, unworthy, gross, a slob, etc. even though none of these are based in fact and are, more often than not, far from the truth).

We'll dive deeper into this later in the book, but for now, I define body neutrality as a feeling of neutrality regarding one's body—not feeling too strongly for or against one's bodily appearance, capabilities, or faculties.

Lastly, let's talk about why I define body positivity as a white-washed, thin-washed buzzword that used to represent what body liberation now represents. When body positivity was first used by activists years ago, it was as a way to uplift those in bodies that didn't conform to "the norm". However, it soon became conflated with self-love, body-love, and body acceptance—all terms that are extremely important in singular people's journeys to body love but not indicative of a social justice movement to free marginalized bodies from oppression. If you go back to the years between 2015 and 2017 on social media, you will see the change in bodies represented under the hashtags and the displacement of fat, brown bodies for thinner, whiter bodies.

Questions to Answer Now

What is your knowledge of weight stigma, body liberation, body positivity, and body-based oppression after reading how I have defined them for you?

Now, knowing better what these terms mean, in what ways have you directly experienced or been affected by body-based oppression in your lifetime?

Additional Materials to Peruse:

I want to remind you that you are in charge here. You're most likely an adult and know this anyway, but there was a time when I sought out permission to live my life according to new rules, so I am giving you unconditional permission, once again, to take what you want from this program and leave the rest. Everything in this book is optional and up to you whether you choose to complete it—however, I do highly recommend at least reading the social posts and one or two of the first books on the list, if possible.

A good way to pace yourself is to read the social posts now and read the other books after you finish this book. If you're a less voracious physical or digital book reader, then many of these books are also available as audiobooks. Or you can also choose to watch some of the TV shows, instead.

The last caveat is that, depending on where you are in your journey away from diet culture and internalized anti-fat bias, some of these may seem groundbreaking, or they may be basic. Either way, it's up to you to decide what you feel you need to read, when you need to read it, or what parts you skip through.

(🔗 **Remember, all the links are available at the site linked to the QR code at the beginning of the book and at the back of the book.**)

Social Posts

- ✳ Body Image is Not the Same As...
- ✳ What Body Image Actually Is...
- ✳ Body Neutrality
- ✳ Weight Loss is Not the Solution
- ✳ Why "Fat" Became a Bad Word

* Black + Brown Bodies and Eating Disorders
* Fat is an Access Issue

Book List

* *Dietland* by Sarai Walker
* *Fearing the Black Body* by Sabrina Strings
* *What We Don't Talk About When We Talk About Fat* by Aubrey Gordon
* *Fat Talk* by Virginia Sole-Smith
* *Anti-Diet* by Christy Harrison, MPH, RD
* *Belly of the Beast* by Da'Shaun Harris

Articles - ***TW: because the Ob*sity slur may be used***

* "Weight Discrimination: A Socially Acceptable Injustice" By Rebecca Puhl
* "Yes, You Can Still Be Fired for Being Fat" By Josh Eidelson
* "Fat Is Not the Problem—Fat Stigma Is" By Lindo Bacon, Amee Severson

TV Shows + Movies

* *Dietland*
* *Shrill*
* *Survival of the Thickest*
* *Fattitude*
* *YrFatFriend*

A Wrap-Up Note

⭐Take a moment to write down any feelings that have come up for you in doing the work thus far, whether it is new information or challenging feelings about your body/identity. This is a great time to break in a favorite new pen or pencil and, perhaps, an accompanying digital note in your phone. There are blank note pages at the end of this book so that you have an additional, centralized place to make note of your feelings and/or experiences as you read. This will not only help you to process in the moment but will give you a place to reflect on later down the road.

Introductions + Who Are You? Really...

Introduction: In this section, you should expect to craft an introduction of yourself more comprehensively than just your body + body size. I want to meet you as who you truly and wholeheartedly are. I want to learn where you're at currently, in what ways you might identify with identities outside of fatness or body size, what roles you play in the world, and what forms of oppression you live under or benefit from. This, almost certainly, will feel difficult to write out (potentially easy, though, depending on where you are in your own work). But becoming aware of and incorporating more of your identities into the work you do will truly help inform your work, recovery, and emotional resilience so much more.

We are very complex, humans are. We are made up of various identities (both target identities and agent identities). These identities can be visual or private depending on how we present ourselves and physically show up in the world. Our identities make up our place in the world in terms of how people perceive and interact with us and how we perceive and interact with others. These can lead to internalized and outright oppression and/or prejudice against other identity groups. These identities make up the diagram displayed in the "cage of oppression" by Jona Olsson's anti-oppression work. I will note that, throughout this book, I utilize broader anti-oppression work and diagrams to explain concepts but frequently have to add in body size or fatness because they are not often readily included as a form of systemic oppression. In the cage of oppression, there isn't a space for body size specifically, although "lookism" is included, which I consider inadequate but close enough to a recognized identity.

Jona Olsson's 'Cage of Oppression'[2]

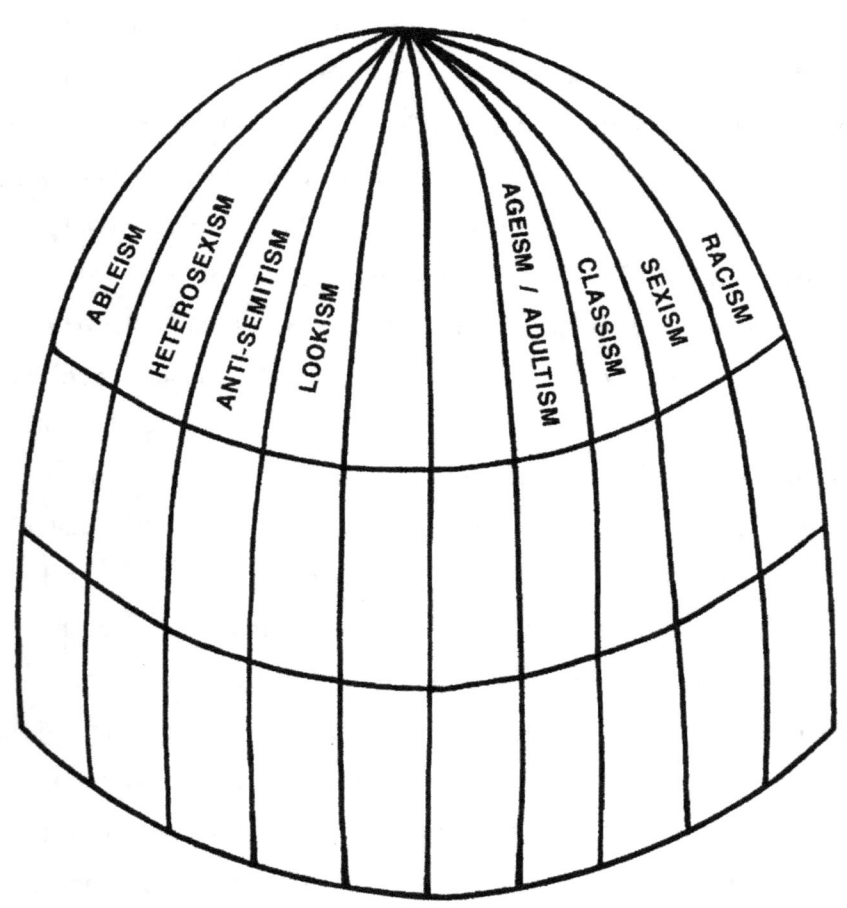

Target and Agent Identities

In this next section, you'll be asked to mark yourself into one of two categories of identities—agent and target identities—so I am giving you the definition of each here, but if you would like to refresh your mind later, you can find them in the Glossary at the end of the book!

The Definition of Target and Agent Identities:

* **An Agent Identity** - Social identity groups that are positioned to be afforded agency, advantaged, dominant, and hold unearned privilege in society.

* **A Target Identity** - Social identity groups that are positioned as targeted by oppression, to be disenfranchised, subordinated, exploited, and/or otherwise harmed.

🧠 **Remember: You're allowed to have any identity if YOU feel it fits and it feels supportive to you to identify that way. No one dictates whether you embody that identity except for you, but also keep in mind the definitions of each identity and in what ways it may or may not apply to you. Maybe you're not feeling comfortable yet holding or owning that identity. Maybe you are. Maybe you choose to wait to make that decision on a later day. All are perfectly okay decisions in this work.**

Which of these described identities do you identify as being an agent identity of, and which do you identify as being a target identity of? How does it feel to identify that way?

* **Race** - A social construct that divides people into separated groups based on characteristics such as physical appearance, cultural identification, cultural history, and ethnic roots. In the case of racial

identity, this would mean that people who are of races that are visibly different from the white race are often discriminated against based on these defining features.

* **Ethnicity** - The quality or fact of belonging to a population group or subgroup made up of people who share a common cultural background or descent. In the case of ethnic identity, this would mean that people who are of ethnicities that are non-American or non-Westernized ethnicities are often discriminated against based on this fact.

* **Sex** - A biological classification based on the physical differences between male, female, and intersex peoples, often rooted in anatomy or physiology. In this case, anyone of a sex not male may be subject to various forms of discrimination based on this fact.

* **Gender/Gender Identity** - A social construct that, oftentimes, relies on the binary behavioral, cultural, and/or psychological traits between men and women. However, in reality, it encompasses a wide variety of genders and gender identities, including identities such as nonbinary, transgender, genderfluid, gender non-conforming, bigender, genderqueer, agender, and so many more amazing genders! Gender is often misconstrued as biological sex, but they are not the same. In this case, anyone of a gender or gender identity that does not align with the traditional binary of men and women may be subject to various forms of discrimination based on this fact.

* **Immigrant/Immigration Experience** - A person who has moved permanently from their native country or place to a new/foreign country. In this case, anyone who has immigrated to a new country

(regardless of whether it is deemed "better" or not) may be subject to various forms of discrimination based on this fact.

* **Religion/Faith** - A set of organized beliefs and/or practices/systems that often dictate the belief and/or worship of a higher force—like a God, Gods, or other supernatural being. I would determine "spirituality" as an agent identity in this identity. In this case, anyone who engages with or practices a religion or spiritual practice outside of traditional, Western religions may be subject to various forms of discrimination based on this fact.

* **Ability** - The experience of living in an able-bodied body and being easily capable of doing something requiring your body. In this case, anyone who lives in a disabled body or a body that is not able-bodied may be subject to various forms of discrimination based on this fact.

* **Non-Visible Disabilities** - A disability that could be physical, mental, or a neurological condition that limits a person's physical or mental ability or activities but is not readily "visible" to those around them. I separate this from general "ability", as this goes further into identity for many people. In this case, those who live in bodies where they have non-visible/invisible disabilities may be subject to various forms of discrimination based on this fact.

* **Sexual Orientation/Sexuality** - An individual's physical, sexual, romantic, and/or emotional attraction to another person. In this case, someone whose sexual orientation goes against the highly socialized "straight" sexuality may be subject to various forms of discrimination based on this fact.

* **Formal Education Level** - The level of formal [Westernized] education completed by the person during their life up to this point. This includes

things like grade school education, secondary education, college education, and post-graduate education. In this case, people who have not completed "enough" formal education may be subject to various forms of discrimination based on this fact—the fact here is that there is never "enough" formal education to escape potential discrimination, in some form.

* **Class** - A system within society that determines and segregates people of various perceived social and/or economic statuses. In this case, people who are of a lower class, or even perceived as part of a lower class, may be subject to various forms of discrimination based on this fact.

* **Age** - The length of time a person has been alive. People alive longer and of a greater age can be exposed to ageism and discrimination based on their age. In this case, anyone of an older age may be subject to various forms of discrimination based on this fact.

* **Lookism** - The creation of a rigid set of standards to define beauty and attractiveness. Several harsh judgments can be made about people based on their ability to meet and maintain these standards. If one doesn't meet these standards, they can be discriminated against based on that fact.

* **Body Size/Fatness** - I am going further than the term "lookism" to add in Body Size/Fatness as its own identity outside of "Pretty Culture". Fat people experience discrimination directly based on their body size and weight that may be, at times, alleviated by being "pretty" but is never truly avoided. So, in this case, someone living with a body that does not look "pretty/hot/beautiful/editorial/straight-sized/thin/skinny/tiny/etc./etc." may be subject to various forms of

Body Size/Fatness/Lookism discrimination based on their body's size and look.

For each of the identities listed below, mark off whether you identify as part of the Target Identity or Agent Identity.

How do You Identify?

AGENT + TARGET IDENTITIES

Race
- ☐ Agent Identity
- ☐ Target Identity

Ethnicity
- ☐ Agent Identity
- ☐ Target Identity

Sex
- ☐ Agent Identity
- ☐ Target Identity

Gender/Gender Identity
- ☐ Agent Identity
- ☐ Target Identity

Immigrant/ Immigration Experience
- ☐ Agent Identity
- ☐ Target Identity

Religion/Faith
- ☐ Agent Identity
- ☐ Target Identity

Ability
- ☐ Agent Identity
- ☐ Target Identity

Non-Visible Disabilities
- ☐ Agent Identity
- ☐ Target Identity

Sexual Orientation/ Sexuality
- ☐ Agent Identity
- ☐ Target Identity

How do You Identify?

AGENT + TARGET IDENTITIES

Formal Education Level

☐ Agent Identity
☐ Target Identity

Class

☐ Agent Identity
☐ Target Identity

Age

☐ Agent Identity
☐ Target Identity

Lookism/ "Prettyness"

☐ Agent Identity
☐ Target Identity

Body Size/Fatness

☐ Agent Identity
☐ Target Identity

Questions to Answer

What factors in your life have led to the development or creation of these identities? Which of these were you born with? Which ones have you come to hold later on in life?

Do any of these identities affect how others see or perceive you in the world? In what ways?

In what ways do your identities affect the choices you make in your life?

Another Diagram of How Identities can Vary in Representation

Before moving on from this activity, I wanted to present one other diagram of identity and how it can vary within each identity. This is a graphic[3] by @sylviaduckworth, which was adapted from ccrweb.ca's original diagram, which you can find in the resources link.

Activity to Complete: Who Are You?

Let's get to know ourselves! For this activity, introduce yourself utilizing any and all of your identities—but try and make it fun or kind of engaging.

You could write out a "Nice to meet you!" kind of social post that you could put on Facebook if you feel bold enough, or you can write out a story introducing yourself to, well... just you. Another cool idea could be to put together a vision board or picture collage where you find elements that identify the pieces of you.

Whatever format feels best and safest for you!

If you want to share this with me, drop it in the Disruptive Dialogue Community, tag me, or send it to me on Instagram @thefriendineverwanted!

Activity to Complete: Tell an Identity Story...

Take a moment to realize where you are with your identities and your representation, or lack of representation, of the ones listed. Look at the identities and questions before again. Now, take the time to jot down something that feels important that comes up when you think about those identities.

These can be sticky/icky feelings, good feelings, or hard feelings. Maybe it's a story you remember from being a kid or a time you were picked on or bullied for that identity. Or, maybe, it's the story of how you've benefited from that identity when someone else didn't.

Write it out below...

Part 1 Wrap-up

You've reached the end of Part 1. Now is a great time to take a moment to write down any feelings, experiences, memories, etc. that have come up for you while doing this work.

Part 2

Meeting and Feeding Your Needs

A NOTE BEFORE YOU HOP IN...

Part of this section may feel super uncomfy, hard, challenging, or difficult. That is okay. *And* if it feels TOO hard or scary in this moment, you are always welcome to skip over it. We will be talking about how we nourish our bodies and take care of our humanistic needs. Some of this can definitely feel triggering, especially if you have lived experience with an eating disorder.

So, while I invite you to read through the instructions for this section, you are free to skip right ahead to the next section in here: Practicing Affirming Self-Talk, if you'd like! And you're also welcome to peruse and then choose to skip ahead later. At no point are you required to complete anything that makes you feel unsafe or triggered.

(⟋ Remember to use the QR code at the beginning or find the links at the back of the book when going through.)

Prioritizing Your Basic Needs? + Picking and Setting Habits

Introduction: In this section, you will become more aware of how things like food, sleep, and self-care are needed in this line of work. You will also learn about setting/practicing habits in a more neurodivergent-friendly way.

Reflecting on Your [Current] Basic Needs:

Chances are, if you're reading this book right now, then you are working through some sort of body image work, self-love work, body liberation work, etc., or you're hoping to learn more about those topics. You're most likely aware of how these directly relate to diet culture, and even disordered eating/eating disorders.

So, if you're also struggling with some form of not consuming enough food for your body's caloric needs due to fear of your body changing, ***you are not alone in this***.

There is so often a co-occurrence between not eating enough and struggling to nourish our bodies adequately as we fight to break through body hatred or self-loathing—to a place of more self-compassion and self-love, and possibly eventually, body neutrality.

And yet, we must be *very* clear that your brain cannot appropriately help you to understand the world and your place in it, do its job to keep your organs and thoughts functioning, as well as support you in making space for yourself in the world, without adequate food and nourishment.

I'm not calling you out here if you're not eating enough. But I am shining a light on the truth of reality.

Now, for this activity. You may be having a flashback to your first dietitian session or even the "food journals" you did in high-school health class—BUT I promise you, this is different. It may sound similar at first, but it's not the same thing.

I am inviting you to reflect on the ways in which you are currently caring for yourself and your body. Think more descriptively than numerically. You don't need to put down numbers at all, even. Just describe the answers to the questions below.

Some of these answers may include thinking and reflecting about the time you spend doing activities like sleeping, drinking liquids, nourishing your body, keeping up with personal hygiene, etc. But still, the exercise isn't meant to "track" things so that you can reach a goal or beat your last best number—the "goal" is to get a clearer understanding of where you stand in these categories.

I am not asking you to track or write down your food intake anywhere

And for the earth signs in the room, *cough* *cough*, I am not in charge of *how* you choose to complete this activity or how you write down the answers to these questions. There is still no "wrong" way to do things, and you are welcome to elaborate as much or as little as you want!

I will present you with some starter/reflection questions to jump-start your thinking about how you might answer these prompts:

Questions to Answer:

🧠 **Remember: There is no judgment here, and whatever you're doing is just as good a place to start as where anyone else is starting their journey from.**

On a given night, how much am I sleeping? Is it consistent? Do I find that I'm waking up throughout the night? Am I taking medication to help me sleep?

How much water/fluid do I generally drink in a day? (Feel free to report in cups, bottles, energy drinks, etc.)

Do I have medication that I need to be taking daily? Do I take my medication daily?

How regularly throughout the day do I experience physical signs/feelings of hunger?

When I experience those signs of hunger, what is my emotional reaction? What is my physical reaction?

When I am hungry, do I readily seek out food to satiate that hunger? Is this food usually emotionally and physically satiating?

How often am I consuming various meals/snacks/etc. in a day?

What sort of food rules do I believe/do I hold on to/do I follow throughout my day?

Do I feel like my relationship with food is completely neutral? Why or why not?

Do I currently make time for daily personal hygiene and care tasks like showering, brushing my teeth, etc.? Why or why not?

Do I struggle to get myself to complete care tasks? How often do I give in? How often do I force myself to do them anyway?

Do I feel better or worse physically, mentally, and emotionally when I complete my care tasks?

Feel free to add in any other answers/questions/thoughts on this topic you have here as well...

Questions About Habits and Your [Past] Experiences:

What do you struggle with most when it comes to picking, setting, and executing new habits?

What specific habits have you tried to set in the past, and how did it go? Why do you think it went that way?

If you have you successfully added habits to your daily life in the past, in what ways did you do it? What didn't work? What did work? How long did you maintain those new habit(s)?

Activity to Complete: "I Want to Make Habits"

You can find this on the next pages.

IDENTIFYING YOUR OWN ACTIVITY PATTERNS

Identify The Best Environmental Stimuli to Keep You Focused:

- Look around and find the best settings for you to be the most focused and productive. Then, identify the conditions that contribute to your best productivity outcomes.

IDENTIFYING YOUR OWN ACTIVITY PATTERNS

Identify The Best Timeframes:

- Try and figure out when you most often feel at your best when it comes to focusing and being productive during the day.
- Pay attention to the specific timeframes when you tend to get the most done.

IDENTIFYING YOUR OWN ACTIVITY PATTERNS

Orient Your New Habits Around Timeframes Or Stimuli That Already Exist For You Like:

- Your morning coffee, getting out of bed and going to the bathroom, taking the dogs out, eating breakfast, going to work, etc...

EMBRACE VARIETY IN HOW YOU APPROACH CONSISTENCY

How to Reintroduce Yourself to Your Old Goals:

- Our brains crave variety and newness to maintain focus, and at the same time they need consistency and structure for functionality.
- We have to balance both needs to succeed!
- Look around and find the best settings for you to be the most focused and productive. Then identify the conditions that contribute to your best productivity outcomes.

- **How can you change the rewards of your old habit to make them new?**

- **How can you break a bigger habit into smaller, more defined tasks?**

- **Can you set new alarms for old tasks that sound new and novel?**

- **In what ways can you take the old, stale interference that blocks you from doing that habit/task and remove it or overcome it?**

REDEFINE YOUR RELATIONSHIP WITH HOW YOU SEE ROUTINES

Cut Down On The Size Of The Task To Make It Easier To Accomplish:

- When just about any task becomes *repetitive* and loses its appeal.
- To counter this, start by trying to break the behavior, task, or habit into smaller increments. Instead of committing to an hour-long activity, start with doing just one minute and then gradually increase it. This approach helps the brain to adopt the new habit more effectively.

- **In what ways can you cut the big task up into micro-tasks that make them much easier to do?**

- **If you try doing the microtask and it still feels "too big", is it possible to make it even smaller?**

- **What habits do you have that feel too large currently to take on? How can you turn them into microtasks?**

- **With those new microtasks, can you scatter them around your day or week to achieve them more easily?**

PICK OUT BOTH YOUR INTERNAL AND EXTERNAL MOTIVATORS

What Motivators Exist Internally To You That You Can Use To Get Excited About Doing The Habit?

- Examples would be: Why did you choose to make this a habit for yourself? What do you want to achieve by making this change in your behavior or life? Are these beliefs enough to keep you engaging in that habit change?

PICK OUT BOTH YOUR INTERNAL AND EXTERNAL MOTIVATORS

What Motivators Exist Externally To You That You Can Use To Get Excited About Doing The Habit?

- Examples would be: Are there others around you who would also like to make this habitual change? Can you set appointments with others so you have to show up and engage with them? What other forms of accountability outside of you and yourself exist?

Wrap-up Questions:

As you come to the end of this section, take a moment to write down any feelings that have come up for you. Was there any new information or a new feeling that felt challenging to hold or understand? Did you feel like pushing back against any suggestions or solutions presented to you?

Practicing Affirming Self-Talk

Introduction: *It's hard to talk positively about ourselves! So, this week, we'll be breaking down a personal affirmation to use and discussing how we can speak more positively in a way that doesn't feel fake or unreal.*

A turning point in my own recovery when I went from feeling very out of control with my own treatment to feeling more in charge of my recovery came at the request of a therapist for me to develop my own affirmation. I'm sure many of us know how beneficial it can be to practice positive affirmations + positive self-talk when we speak about ourselves—and if you weren't aware yet, go ahead and check out this article, "Neuroplasticity and How Rewiring is Important to Recovery"[4] on the benefits of creating new neural pathways in our brains that run on positive self-talk as opposed to negative self-talk. Chances are, if you know about these things, you also know how challenging it can be to keep up with that positive self-talk and not let it slide back into critical thoughts about ourselves. If you've tried to engage in positive self-talk in the past and did end up slipping back into critiquing yourself, you did not fail, and you were not, not successful—you likely weren't going slow enough and weren't focusing on making one small shift at a time.

When I started prioritizing positive-self talk in my life, I started with one simple affirmation: "I am okay". When I felt things getting out of control, I would repeat this to myself, almost like a mantra, and then I would say it 10 times over, hoping to blast away any negative feelings. It didn't immediately make everything okay; no, it did not. But after a while of utilizing this mantra and repeating it to myself throughout the day, I started to notice that when things got really hard, I felt on edge, or I was having a hard time. I would comfort myself by repeating "I'm okay" over and over. It made it to a point where I would say it to myself and know it to be true because I was okay and things were going to be okay.

Activity to Complete: Your Personal Affirmation

We're going to spend this activity time developing your own personal affirmation that you can use, recite, and practice when things feel hard or out of control. Honestly, you can use it whenever you want! But I highly recommend having it on hand for situations where a feeling of comfort or validation would be especially helpful.

So, in this activity, we are prioritizing the practice of positive self-talk by first coming up with an affirmation that feels true to us deep down and that we know we need to hear. If you do inner child work, this might be a phrase your inner child really, really needs to hear. And if you *don't* do inner child work, that's perfectly okay, too. It may be the opposite of a phrase you usually use to critique yourself.

Fun fact: the brain doesn't know the difference between you "meaning it" when you recite positive affirmations, so even if you're faking it until you make it, the faking it *actually* works... so keep it up!

Questions to Determine Your Affirmation

What is a point in your life currently where you feel you tend to critique yourself or "yell" at yourself for not succeeding, living up to expectations, etc.?

Does that time when you feel like you've let yourself down mirror a time in the past when you let someone else down for something similar? Yes? No? If so, who was it, and how was it handled?

How do you feel in those moments when you've let yourself (or someone else) down? What is your physical or emotional reaction to the feeling of letting yourself (or that other person) down?

What is an alternative way you would want to feel if you could snap your fingers and change your feelings/thoughts immediately? What other option would you choose?

What would that sound like/feel like to you in the moment after the change?

If someone came to you with the exact issue you're having now—letting someone down, not doing their "best", feeling let down, etc.—what would you tell them to get them to understand what you see in them? What would you say to get them to reach that alternative way of thinking that you, yourself, are wishing for?

Can you simplify that down to a sentence or phrase? What would it be?

Write out your personal affirmation below...

Now, the next step is to put this affirmation into practice as much as you can. Write it down, say it to yourself when you're driving, repeat it when you're in the shower; however, you practice it is A-OKAY with me.

Regardless of how or when you decide to practice your affirmation, here are some ways to reflect or take notice of how it's going:

* Notice when you remember that your affirmation even exists.
* Notice when you choose to use your affirmation.
* Notice what sort of feelings come up when you say it.
* Do you feel silly? Inspired? Exhausted? Annoyed? These are all SUPER valid feelings.
* Do you repeat it more than once, or just say it quickly and forget about it again?

Wrap-up Questions:

As you come to the end of this section, reflect on the activities and questions in this section. Write down any feelings that have come up for you in doing the work thus far. How are things feeling thus far? Are you frustrated with the work in this book? The questions? The activities? What feelings are coming up for you?

Evaluate Your Life + Habit Setting for Better Self-Care

Introduction: In this section, you will be making a plan to implement a couple of habits over the next few weeks that will, ideally, promote self-care, body neutrality, or some other area of your life that feels helpful!

We will be walking through a [Nia] revised version of the Level 10 Life[5] activity—and, in my opinion, a *better* version. I'm not sure if you've already encountered the Level 10 Life activity, but one of my main "beefs" with it is that there is an idea that all parts of your life can or should be at "level 10" all at once—like that that's the goal. At least, it was the first time someone taught it to me, and I didn't even know I was neurodivergent then. So, in my reality, we know that life gets in the way and things come up, and sometimes your family has to be your priority, or sometimes finances have to be your priority. The assumption that all these areas of your life can be at a 10/10 at one time feels very neurotypical. Anyways... let's dive into an altered version of the activity.

Activity to Complete: Level 10 Life

The directions to complete the activity are on the next page. But first, the guidelines:

Level 10 Life Activity Guidelines to Apply:

First, on the worksheet, you will find that there are 6 major areas of your life that you will (or can) assess yourself on, including:

* *Finances:* money, wealth, assets, donations, charity, tithing, etc.

* *Health:* physical health, mental health, movement, medication, chronic illness, disability, physical freedom, nourishment, etc. (you can define "health" however you want to)

* *Relationships:* love, family, friends, dating, nesting partners, polyamory, BDSM dynamics, coworkers, social life, kids, fur babies, etc.

* *Home:* comfort, stability, location, feeling safe, home social life, satisfaction, etc.

* *Career & Education:* level of education, level of career/work, time spent, work-life balance, satisfaction, niche + industry, dream fulfillment, etc.

* *Spirituality:* religion, organized worship, time spent, tarot, witchyness, connection with the divine, connection with god, belief systems, meditation, spiritual nourishment, etc. (you can define this how you would like to)

Step 1:

Fill out the sections for each area of your life with the things that are currently taking up space in that area.

* For example, if you are currently married or dating, you might want to list that under the "Relationships" section.

* Another example is if you're currently going through cancer treatment, and it is having an impact on your life (which would be expected), you would list this under "Health". But also, maybe, under "Finances" if the cost of treatment influences your life.

Step 2:

Gauge these life sections for yourself **currently** by filling in the pie chart on the worksheet.

* For example, if finances are on the high end of your budget but you want to focus on reducing them or finding a way to finance them---that may be noted as a lower "score" on the wheel. But, if you are checking your accounts, budgeting every day, and living within your means---that score may be closer to a "10" for you.

🌑 **Remember: you don't have to do this activity "correctly", and that there's no real "right answer" here. You are simply giving yourself an idea of what areas of your life you'd like to focus more heavily on at the moment.**

Step 3:

Take the areas of your life where you're feeling a lack of organization or a lack of asserted control (like keeping up with your to-do list or making it to appointments on time, etc.) and jot down some ideas about what small steps you could take to give yourself more structure in those areas of life.

* For example, reading and engaging with this book could go under mental health work, therefore health—and so a small action would be taking 5-15 minutes/day to work on this material.

* You'll want to have at least a few examples of habits you can implement over the next several weeks that you feel may move the needle for one or more of these categories of life.

Some things to consider when narrowing down your life of habits:

* Can you **stack** any of those habits with things you already do? For me, I always stack brushing my teeth onto showering because showering will happen but brushing my teeth won't always. So, every time I shower, I know my teeth will also get brushed.

* Can you set an alarm to remind you to make time for that habit on a consistent schedule?

* Can you involve another human in your plan to help remind you to do the habit? OR, can you stack your habit onto something that they do so that when they do their thing, you're reminded to do yours?

* Can you make the activity more exciting/novel by jamming out to new music on your phone or listening to an audiobook so you get more dopamine from the boring/must-do-life activity but also still get it done?

* I can't wait to see your habit list and see how you approach prioritizing them!

Step 4:

Come back to this activity at the end of the book—or in a month or two or three—and re-gauge these life levels for yourself at that time using the second page of the worksheet.

Level 10 Life

WORKSHEET

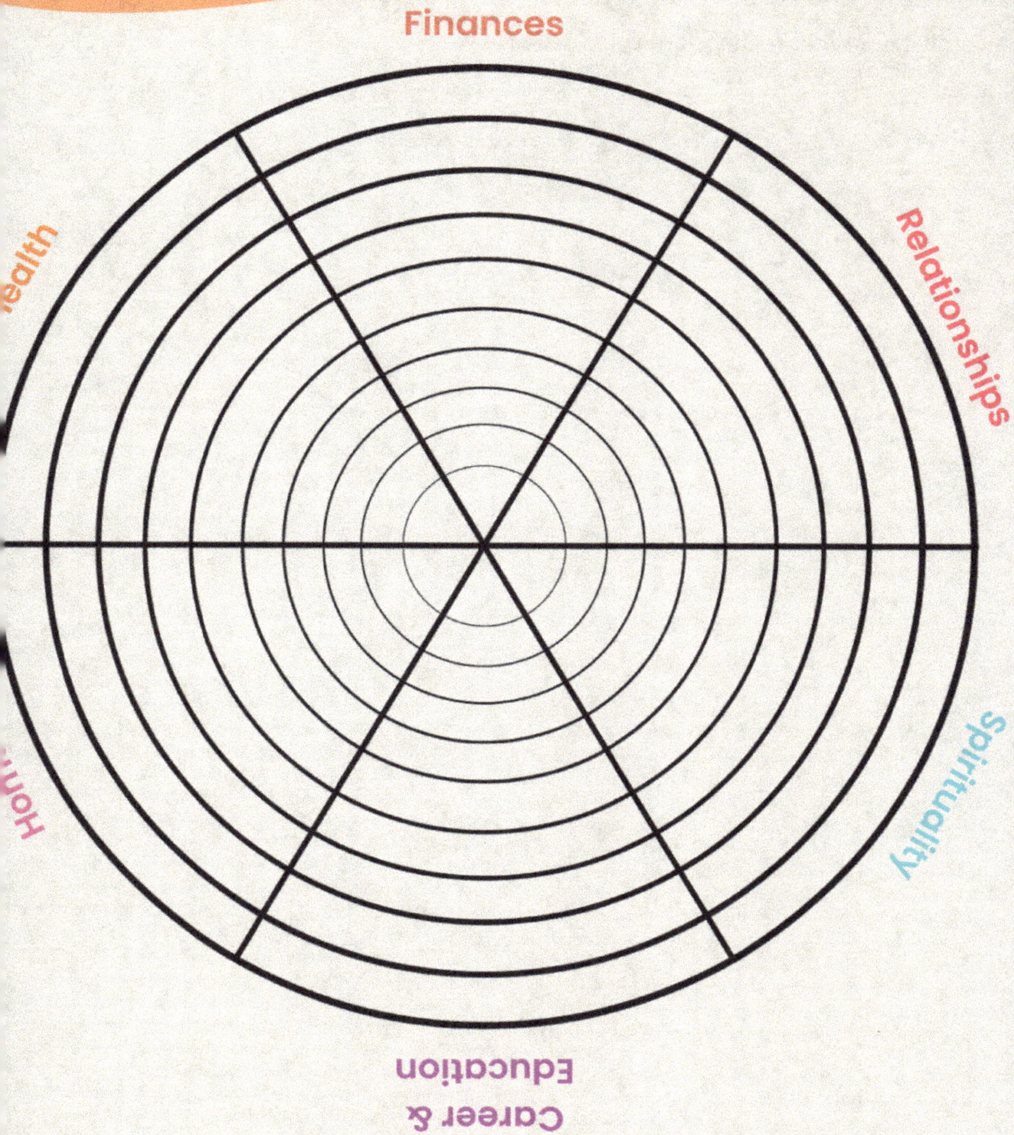

Finances

Relationships

Spirituality

Career & Education

Health

Home

Wrap-up Questions:

Hello! You're doing amazing! Now that you've reached the end of this section, you are just about ready to start Part 3! But before you do, take a moment and reflect on the activities and questions in the previous section. Write down any feelings that have come up for you in doing the work thus far. How are things feeling? Are you frustrated with the work in this book? The questions? The activities? What feelings are coming up for you?

Part 3

Challenging The Fear of Fatness

A NOTE BEFORE YOU HOP IN...

Part 3 is where the "meat" of this book's work is done. It's heavy, it's deep, and it may call up lots of feelings that you've been stuffing down for a while. I very much know that this is a possibility, and even a likelihood. But I ask you to not skip over it, not go around it, but go straight through it.

But I am here with you 100% of the way; picture me holding your hand and wearing a light-up bodysuit-illuminating the way forward for us!

We will be getting mighty uncomfortable in this part, but you're ready for it. You've made it thus far already, and I know that you are as prepared as can be to go through.

And, if you're feeling TOO uncomfy or unable to move forward in this work, take a break, put this book down, step back, and take a pause. Talk with the people you trust so that you feel heard, taken seriously, and cared for so that you can better move forward if you choose to.

(🔗 Remember to use the QR code at the beginning or find the links at the back of the book when going through.)

Labeling Your Fat Fears + Body-Based Heartache

Introduction: We don't talk about our own fear of being fat or becoming fatter often. In this step, we will dig deeper into what may be holding you back from accepting your body as-is or, at least, forming a neutral outlook toward it. We will also look at what is so "scary" to you about being fat or gaining weight. Lastly, we will dig into the grief of losing the dream body or dream life that came with that dream body, letting that dream go and replacing it with a new dream that you can strive for in your current body.

Labeling Your Fear of Fat

Earlier this year, I posted this Instagram post, and it resonated with several people—me very much included as well. It is so important to note that, while we are working to accept our bodies and change our outlook on them, the world isn't necessarily doing its own work on this topic at the same time. Yes, the world can, at times, be outright hostile to fat people.

"I don't know how to be neutral towards a body [that] society is not neutral towards."

@THEFRIENDINEVERWANTED

And so, if you are a fat human being in this world, then chances are you have developed a fear of being fat in this society. How could you not? It's normal to fear fatness. It's normal to fear ridicule and disgust from the world—this dislike and avoidance of "othering" is what it is to be a human. **AND yet, we cannot do this work, we** cannot show up for ourselves, without looking fatness in the face and embracing it. So, let's talk about you now...

Questions to Answer and Reflect on:
What feeling comes up when you hear the word "fat"?

What fears come up when you think about existing in a fat body (if you don't already)? Or, if you do exist in a fat body already, what fears come up when you picture yourself in a public space, just existing?

Have you ever been bullied, ridiculed, harassed, insulted, or attacked for being fat?

If so, how did that feel? If not, why do you think that is?

Where do you feel closest to right now in terms of your relationship with your body?

A Spectrum of Body Acceptance

Breaking Down the Body Acceptance Spectrum

I actually created the below graphic of the Body Acceptance Spectrum that represents a common trajectory from not being aware of your relationship with your body through several different parts of the spectrum and where you may [want to] end up.

Now, let's dive into each of the spots on the spectrum and what they might mean or look like for someone.

Body Love:

You love your body just as it is today and every day, even when it changes, even when things don't go perfectly. As with all relationships of love, things don't always turn out exactly right, and it's not like there isn't rupture or tension, but you feel confident enough to work through that with your body and move on from it rather quickly.

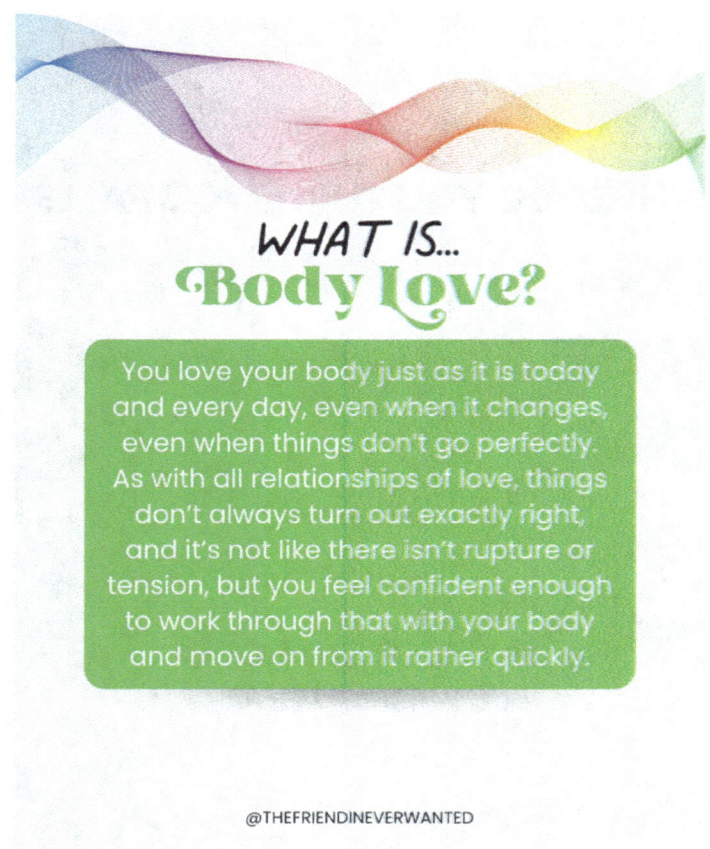

WHAT IS...
Body Love?

You love your body just as it is today and every day, even when it changes, even when things don't go perfectly. As with all relationships of love, things don't always turn out exactly right, and it's not like there isn't rupture or tension, but you feel confident enough to work through that with your body and move on from it rather quickly.

@THEFRIENDINEVERWANTED

Body Neutrality:

You may not love your body, but you also don't hate it. Maybe you did at one point. But right now, you're feeling rather neutral about it. You acknowledge that things may be harder in your body or not ideal, but you don't let those feelings trip you up too badly. You're still standing your ground. It's not a "I love my body" celebration every day, but some days it might be, and some days you might scowl and feel utterly frustrated about how your body feels. But overall, there is a balance that evens out in a sense of neutrality toward your body.

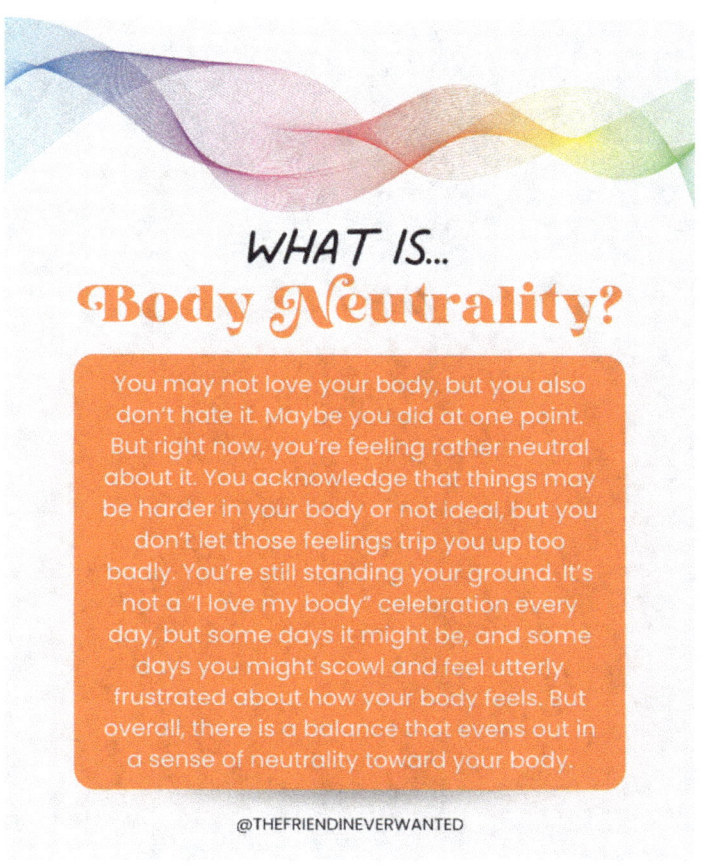

WHAT IS...
Body Neutrality?

You may not love your body, but you also don't hate it. Maybe you did at one point. But right now, you're feeling rather neutral about it. You acknowledge that things may be harder in your body or not ideal, but you don't let those feelings trip you up too badly. You're still standing your ground. It's not a "I love my body" celebration every day, but some days it might be, and some days you might scowl and feel utterly frustrated about how your body feels. But overall, there is a balance that evens out in a sense of neutrality toward your body.

@THEFRIENDINEVERWANTED

Body Tolerance:

You are actively working to shove down your feelings about your body, or at least sip them slowly. You often feel frustrated by your body, even angry, but you're able to put it aside or logically reason with yourself about why that is and not let it ruin how your day is going. You're putting up with things. You're grinning and bearing it. You're doing okay, but you also still want to actively change your body most days. You wish for a chance to skip out on the body love journey and just go back to restricting and, maybe, dieting altogether—but you also know that won't actually help. Instead, you're here, feeling kinda stuck.

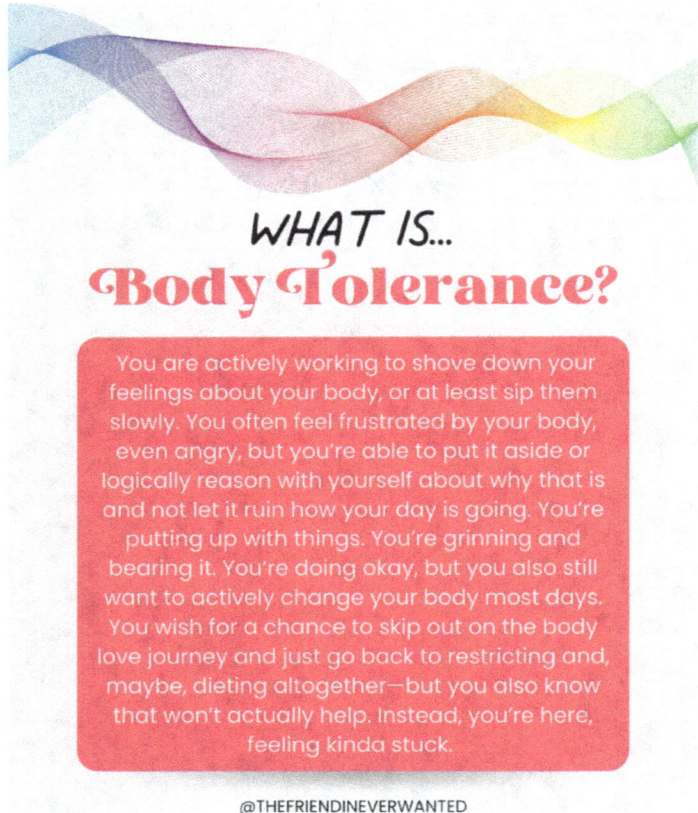

WHAT IS...
Body Tolerance?

You are actively working to shove down your feelings about your body, or at least sip them slowly. You often feel frustrated by your body, even angry, but you're able to put it aside or logically reason with yourself about why that is and not let it ruin how your day is going. You're putting up with things. You're grinning and bearing it. You're doing okay, but you also still want to actively change your body most days. You wish for a chance to skip out on the body love journey and just go back to restricting and, maybe, dieting altogether—but you also know that won't actually help. Instead, you're here, feeling kinda stuck.

@THEFRIENDINEVERWANTED

Body Hatred:

You actively hate your body. You wish you didn't feel such strong feelings about your body, but you do, and it's on your mind constantly. Every time you bump into someone or feel like you're encroaching on another human's space, you tear yourself down—or, at least, begin to. You don't speak too nicely to your body, and your body knows you don't like it. You're not friends with your body, even in a mild sense. You want out, NOW. And you're not opposed to taking more aggressive measures to get there.

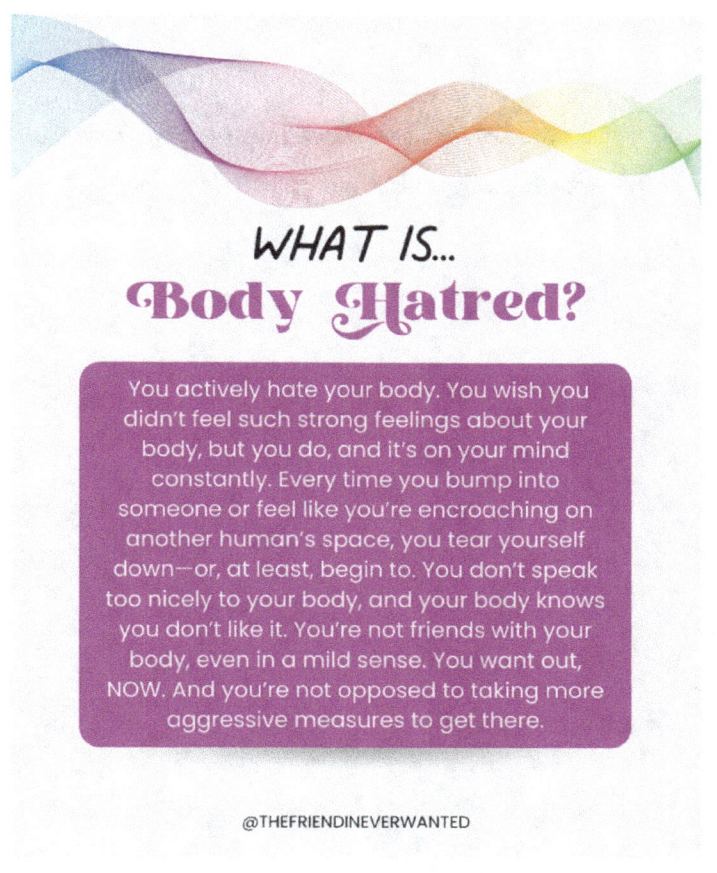

WHAT IS...
Body Hatred?

You actively hate your body. You wish you didn't feel such strong feelings about your body, but you do, and it's on your mind constantly. Every time you bump into someone or feel like you're encroaching on another human's space, you tear yourself down—or, at least, begin to. You don't speak too nicely to your body, and your body knows you don't like it. You're not friends with your body, even in a mild sense. You want out, NOW. And you're not opposed to taking more aggressive measures to get there.

@THEFRIENDINEVERWANTED

Questions for if you're in a spot of Body Neutrality currently...

* When I bring up the idea of body love or "loving your body as it is", what feelings come up for you?

* What would that type of body love mean to you? What would it look like in your wildest dreams?

* Do you feel capable of achieving body love from where you are currently? How far away does it feel to you right now?

<u>Questions for if you're in a spot of Body Tolerance currently...</u>

* When I tell you that you have an opportunity to feel "neutral" toward your body—how it looks, how it feels, how it works—how does that make you feel?

* What would that type of neutrality mean to you? What would it look like in your wildest dreams?

* Do you feel capable of achieving body neutrality from where you are currently? How far away does it feel to you right now?

Questions for if you're in a spot of Body Hatred currently...

* *When I bring up the idea of body tolerance or just making space to "tolerate" your body how it is now, what feelings come up for you?*

* *What would that type of body tolerance mean to you? What would it look like in your wildest dreams?*

* *Do you feel capable of achieving body tolerance from where you are currently? What about body neutrality? How far away does it feel to you right now?*

Overall Questions About Where You Are on the Spectrum:

What steps do you feel like you could take to reach that next level of forming a better relationship with your body?

What do you think is getting in the way between you and that next level right now? What's holding you back from taking the steps you just outlined above?

What do you think body love or body neutrality feels like? What does it look like? Does that feeling and appearance apply to you or just to others?

What would a life when you've "arrived" at body tolerance be like? Does that feel like what you want in your life?

What would a life when you've "arrived" at body neutrality be like? Does that feel like what you want in your life?

What would a life when you've "arrived" at body love be like? Does that feel like what you want in your life?

If it is or isn't what you specifically want in your life, what DO you want your relationship with your body to look like? Feel like?

How would the ways that you treat your body and work alongside your body change when you reach this destination? How would they develop during the journey to that ultimate relationship?

Do you feel capable of treating your body now the way you hope to treat your body later down the road?

Wrap-up Questions:

Now that you've reached the end of this mini-section, you can take a moment to reflect on the information relayed to you in the previous section. Write down any feelings that have come up for you in doing the work thus far. How are things feeling? Are you frustrated with the work in this book? The questions? The activities? What feelings are coming up for you?

What's so Scary about Fatness, Anyway?

Let's jump into this. You wouldn't be here if there weren't some feelings of fear holding you back from accepting your body and having a neutral to positive relationship with your body. We can acknowledge that some things that may also be holding you back are disability or limited mobility, chronic illness, or mental health struggles; however, chances are, if you're reading this book, then there is a fear of fatness that is affecting you. Please fill out the questions below.

Questions to Answer:

What things in your life is "fatness" holding you back from?

In what ways is "fatness" holding you back from those things?

What would happen if you did them or tried them, regardless of what your body looks or is like?

Does fatness inherently "scare" you? As in, do you feel as though fat people are incapable of living a happy, fulfilled life?

Where did this story of what "fatness" means to you now originally come from?

When was the first time you recall someone bullying or shaming a fat person? What happened in that instance?

What do you think you took away from that experience?

How do you know you took that away from that experience? In what ways has your life shifted because of that experience (and other similar events)?

What would you like to believe about fatness and people in larger bodies (that you don't believe now or don't fully believe now)?

Do you feel capable of reaching this belief? Why or why not?

What would it mean to be fat? What would it mean to be fat and also scared?

Some Further Questions to Consider:

✳   *Would you find community with other fat people?*

✳   *If so, would you feel liberated?*

✳   *If so, would you feel alone?*

✳   *If so, would you confront those fears?*

What Are Your Thoughts on these Questions in Particular?

I feel that we, as fat people, can admit that being fat can, at times, be scary, maybe overwhelming, and sometimes not what we signed up for. A quote that comes to mind from a source I don't often quote (and who is also not fat) is:

"If you can't beat fear, just do it scared." — Glennon Doyle Melton[6]

If we cannot beat fear, if we must take on that fear and live our lives alongside it because living in this fearful place means that we are in bodies that are nourished, as happy as is feasible, advocated for, and taken care of, then maybe we must just do it scared. Maybe there is no way to circumvent the scary feelings altogether, and we can learn how to combat them, soothe ourselves, and grow despite our fears.

▶️ *How does that reality or potential reality feel to you?*
Where does that fear come from?

Wrap-up Questions:

Now that you've reached the end of this mini-section, you can take a moment to reflect on the information relayed to you in the previous section. Write down any feelings that have come up for you in doing the work thus far. How are things feeling? Are you frustrated with the work in this book? The questions? The activities? What feelings are coming up for you?

Grieving That Dream Body...

We have to talk about something VERY real for people embarking on a journey that doesn't include diet culture, dieting, or the pursuit of thinness—grieving and letting go of the dream body you've held onto for so long. I can't say every fat person ever has felt this, but certainly, every fat person I've ever asked if they resonate with the dream of a thin body has felt this. Have you? Have you held onto a dream "thin avatar" throughout your life?

For me, my thin avatar was into running and hiking, liked eating as much pizza as they wanted, and had very long hair. I also had kids that I chased around outside all day, a surprisingly unrealistic non-fear of bugs, and often wore cute graphic tees that had catchy phrases on them. This dream version of myself—this "thin ideal"—was elusive, and yet the most real person I could imagine. I could feel myself embodying their body if I could just wake up in a thin body one day. They felt more real than almost anything else I had encountered. That thin version of me felt more real than a happy, fat version of myself.

I am guessing that you, too, have a thin, ideal version of yourself—a "dream you" that lives in a thin body. In this step, we're going to let them go.

Activity: "Thin Ideal Avatar" & "Authentically You Avatar"

We will start by creating the "Thin Ideal Avatar".

Step 1:

First, outline who this "thin version" of yourself is:

* Go ahead and outline everything that the *thin* and "happy" version of yourself embodies. Some things you might consider:

    o   Physical attributes

    o   Emotional wellness

    o   Spiritual beliefs

    o   Habits

    o   Likes/Dislikes

    o   Activities

    o   Family structure

    o   Physical ability

    o   Mental Health

Note: Not everything has to be positive here! So, if you feel that being in a straight-sized/thin body would mean more mental health struggles or less spiritual connection, feel free to add that in.

* 🎨 Paint as clear a picture of who you feel you *could* be as possible.

Meet Your
"THIN IDEAL AVATAR"

Step 2:

Now, take your list of attributes and characteristics of your "Thin Ideal Avatar" and highlight, circle, etc., the following things in different colors or highlighters, whatever works best for you!

BLUE — Anything you feel is not *actually* isolated to a thin version of yourself (Examples: Likes and dislikes, family structure, habits, relationships, etc.)

ORANGE — Anything you feel is actually *only* capable through conforming to diet culture (Examples: Pant sizes, weight numbers, restrictive eating choices, etc.)

PINK — Anything that is of the utmost importance in your mind to be *truly* happy (Examples: Relationships, emotional wellness, happiness, etc.)

Step 3:

Next, take the characteristics you've written under your "Thin Ideal Avatar" and spend a moment to notice what falls under each of these sections.

* *What characteristics have you written down that are completely isolated by body size/weight?*

* *What characteristics have you written down that are possible in a fat body or a disabled body or the body you've been avoiding?*

* *What characteristics have you written down that you are able to pursue regardless of being in a straight-sized or fat body?*

Step 4:

Now, ask yourself if there is a way you can take one of each of these things and make it possible to include them in your current reality without changing your body or other identities.

Next, we'll create Your "Authentically You Avatar"

Step 5:

Start off by adding to this avatar:

* *Things you want to achieve:*

* *Places you want to go:*

* *Things you want to do:*

* *People you want to meet or have in your relationship orbit:*

* *Foods you want to eat:*

* *Habits you want to take on:*

* *Hobbies you want to try:*

* *How you want your emotional, spiritual, physical, and mental needs to be met:*

Step 6:

Now, for a few follow-up questions:

✳ *If you included these in your life, would you be "happy", or some approximation of happier?*

✳ *Would this happiness be dependent on your body's size?*

Step 7:

Take a moment to read through what makes up your "Authentically You Avatar." Does it sound more "you" than your "Thin Ideal Avatar"?

✳ *What impact does the answer to this question have on you?*

✳ *Is this the answer you wanted? Why or why not?*

✳ *What does this answer mean for you?*

Wrap-up Questions:

Now that you've reached the end of this mini-section, you can take a moment to reflect on the major activity we just did in this section. Write down any feelings that have come up for you in doing the work thus far. How are things feeling? Are you frustrated with the work in this book? The questions? The activities? What feelings are coming up for you?

Fighting Internalized Fat Shame

In this section, we will look at and carefully break down what we experience in the world as internalized fat shame and internalized anti-fat bias. We examine what we think of ourselves and what that critical little voice inside our heads really sounds like.

Digging Deeper into Internalized Fatphobia

In college, I sat through several 3-hour intergroup dialogue courses where we looked, in depth, at racism, sexism, colorism, and so many other systems of oppression. Therefore, when creating this book, I took what I had previously learned about systems of oppression and modified them to apply to fat folx and fat bodies, as they, too, experience systems of oppression—though this oppression is not laid out so plainly in literature.

Internalized inferiority, or fatphobic oppression, is just ONE of the foundations of a fatphobic society built on weight stigma.

So, here I am, presenting it to you as I see it:

The 7 Tennent's of Fatphobia + Anti-Fat Bias, which include:

1. Fat people are taught to carry internalized negative messages about themselves and other fat people.
2. Fat people, inherently, are taught to believe there is something wrong with being a fat person.
3. Fat people almost always develop lowered self-esteem and a sense of inferiority and wrongness about themselves and other fat people.
4. Fat people oftentimes have lowered expectations and limited belief in their sense of self-potential.
5. Fat people experience a lack of options or choices regarding how to show up in the world: either lose weight to "assimilate" or "act out" and remain fat (ESPECIALLY being fat and happy).
6. Fat people often have a limited sense of what feels possible and what is possible for them to achieve—which is vastly limited by real and perceived oppression and prejudice.
7. The effect these tenants have on fat people and the internalized beliefs they cause can lead to cycles throughout future generations.

Why does any of this even matter outside of an academic lesson on fatphobia and anti-fatness? Hold on, and I'll tell you! But first, let's look at these two points next...

Here are some of the *negative* messages *fat people* may receive due to explicit and internalized fatphobia:

* In a fatphobic system, the dominant culture (here, thin and straight-sized people) regularly sends fat people *negative* messages about who we are—both individually and as a community.

* Fat people, as a whole, are inevitably shaped by these images, values, norms, standards, beliefs, attitudes, and feelings that presume the dominant group is who we are to be measured against in regard to these *negative* messages.

* Some of the *negative* messages about who fat people "are" may include (but are not limited to): Lazy, Ignorant, Slobs, Underachieving, High Risk, Unhygienic, Mascots, Clowns, Unworthy, Broken, Bad people, Insignificant, Promiscuous, Inadequate, Poor, Criminal, Inferior.

These are some of the *positive* messages that *thin/straight-sized people* may receive due to explicit and internalized fatphobia:

* In a fatphobic system, the dominant culture (here, thin and straight-sized people) regularly receives these *positive* messages about who they are—both individually and as a community.

* Fat people, as a whole, are inevitably shaped by these images, values, norms, standards, beliefs, attitudes, and feelings that presume the dominant group is who we are to be measured against in regard to these *positive* messages.

* Some of the *positive* messages about who thin/straight-sized people "are" may include (but are not limited to): Better, Moral, Individual, Qualified, Smart, Pretty, The "norm", The standard, Leaders, Safe, Deserving, Entitled, Objective, Rational, Justified, Innocent.

What this does mean is that fatphobia and anti-fatness is much, much more complex, and insidious than most people know of or expect. In reality, fat and thin/straight-sized people are both affected by fatphobia BUT, in different ways. It's not so much that thin people are "thin-shamed" for their bodies that means they are affected by fatphobia but the ways in which they are portrayed as upholding the positive messages of fatphobia. This is similar to telling women that sexism doesn't exist because... "Hey! This woman makes more than all the men at her company!" Nope. Try again.

In a fatphobia system there is much more afoot than the system lets us know or allows us to see. Even when we think we understand what's going on we don't see the other layers beneath the surface. This is why when I tell that you being at odds with your body is NOT your fault, I mean it. And you have to see it too. Buying into body hatred is giving our capitalistic society EXACTLY what it wants!

So, tell me, what are you taking away from the 7 Tennent's of Fatphobia + Anti-Fat Bias?

And now, what are you taking away from the breakdown of the negative and positive messages that fat and thin/straight-sized people experience?

What should other people around you learn from this and take away from these two facts?

Activity: Your Internalized Fatphobia Inventory

In this activity, I will walk you through something I've created called an Internalized Fatphobia Inventory. It is based on similar inventories for identities such as race, but in this case, it was created to hone in on aspects specific to fat bias, weight stigma, and body size.

Take an Inventory of your own internalized fatphobia on the next page...

DO I TRUST FAT PEOPLE? DO I EVER REACT TO FAT PEOPLE IN WAYS THAT INDICATE SUSPICION OR MISTRUST?

IN MY WORK OR EDUCATIONAL EXPERIENCE, DO I SEEK OUT APPROVAL FROM THIN/STRAIGHT-SIZED INDIVIDUALS FOR A JOB WELL DONE OVER THAT OF OTHER FAT PEOPLE?

DO I/HAVE I EVER BEEN EMBARRASSED TO RESPOND TO ANOTHER FAT PERSON IN A SITUATION WHERE IT MAY SEEM THAT I AM COLLUDING WITH THEM OR ENCOURAGING THEM TO EMBRACE THEIR FATNESS?

DO I/HAVE I HESITATED TO PARTICIPATE IN VARIOUS EVENTS FOR FEAR OF BEING IDENTIFIED AS SOMEONE WHO MAY BE "GLORIFYING FATPHOBIA" OR "SUPPORTING FATNESS"?

AM I A HARSHER CRITIC OF THE CHOICES OR BEHAVIORS OF OTHER FAT PEOPLE THAN I AM OF THIN/STRAIGHT-SIZED PEOPLE?

WHEN CHOOSING A HEALTHCARE PROVIDER OR OTHER PROVIDER OF SERVICES THAT REQUIRES SPECIFIC EDUCATIONAL TRAINING (I.E. ATTORNEY, EDUCATOR, ETC.) AM I LESS LIKELY TO SELECT A FAT PERSON VERSUS A THIN/STRAIGHT-SIZED PERSON?

HAVE I/DO I INTEND TO ALTER MY PHYSICAL FEATURES IN ANY WAY THAT WILL HIDE OR OBSCURE MY OWN FATNESS/FAT FEATURES?

WHEN CHOOSING A PLACE TO LIVE, WOULD I PREFER TO LIVE WITHIN A COMMUNITY THAT IS A COMMUNITY OF FAT PEOPLE OR A PREDOMINATELY THIN/STRAIGHT-SIZED COMMUNITY?

HOW OFTEN DO I REFER TO OTHER FAT PEOPLE AS "LAZY" OR BY SOME OTHER DEROGATORY/DIMINUTIVE TERM?

WHEN CHOOSING BOOKS, TOYS, OR SIMILAR GIFTS FOR THE CHILDREN IN MY LIFE, HOW CONSCIOUS AM I OF IMAGES, SOUNDS, AND EXPERIENCES THAT REFLECT THEIR BODY SIZE/WEIGHT?

IN MY PLACE OF WORK, DO I GIVE MORE CREDIT OR CREDENCE TO THE THOUGHTS AND IDEAS SHARED BY THIN/STRAIGHT-SIZED PEOPLE VERSUS FAT PEOPLE?

DO I BELIEVE FAT PEOPLE WHEN THEY SPEAK UP OR SHARE THEIR STORIES?

HAVE I EVER QUESTIONED WHETHER A [THIN/STRAIGHT-SIZED] COLLEAGUE OR [THIN/STRAIGHT-SIZED] SERVICE PROVIDER WAS CHOSEN FOR THEIR POSITION BASED ON THEIR BODY SIZE OR APPROXIMATION TO PRIVILEGE?

WHEN CHOOSING SOURCES OF ENTERTAINMENT (LITERATURE, MOVIES, MUSIC, ETC.), HOW OFTEN DO I CHOOSE ART CREATED/PRODUCED BY FAT PEOPLE?

HOW OFTEN AM I EMBARRASSED BY OR DISGUSTED BY OTHER FAT PEOPLE?

HOW OFTEN DO I MISTRUST MY OWN THINKING OR CARRY AROUND DOUBTS ABOUT OTHER FAT PEOPLE'S ABILITY TO THINK WELL?

DO I EVER ACTIVELY OR PASSIVELY BELIEVE OR SUPPORT FAT STEREOTYPES ABOUT MY OWN BODY SIZE GROUP (FOR EXAMPLE: LAUGH AT A FAT JOKE)?

HOW OFTEN DO I OVERCOMPENSATE — ACTIVELY GO OUT OF MY WAY TO CONTRADICT OR DISPROVE A STEREOTYPE THAT I THINK THIN/STRAIGHT-SIZED PEOPLE MAY BE HOLDING ABOUT ME OR OTHER FAT PEOPLE?

AM I EVER ASHAMED OF FAT PEOPLE? HOW OFTEN DO I FEEL ASHAMED OF OR AVOID THOSE WHOSE BODIES ARE "TOO FAT" OR WHO DRESS IN "NOT GOOD ENOUGH" CLOTHING?

DO I EVER CENSOR MY OWN OPINION OR PASSION, OR HESITATE TO MAKE WAVES WHEN MY KNOWLEDGE AND EXPERIENCE ARE OVERLOOKED IN A CONVERSATION, DISCUSSION, OR ARGUMENT WITH THIN/STRAIGHT-SIZED PEOPLE?

HAVE I EVER THOUGHT ABOUT FAT PEOPLE AS "WE ARE OUR OWN WORST ENEMIES"?

HOW OFTEN DO I DOUBT MYSELF? OR SECOND GUESS MYSELF?

DO I PUT ON A DIFFERENT PERSONA WHEN I GO INTO THIN/STRAIGHT-SIZED PEOPLE'S BUSINESSES, ORGANIZATIONS, OR HOMES?

HOW OFTEN AM I UNSUPPORTIVE OF A FAT PERSON'S LEADERSHIP? HAVE I EVER UNDERMINED OR SABOTAGED THEIR LEADERSHIP?

DO I HOLD FAT PEOPLE TO A HIGHER STANDARD THAN I HOLD THIN/STRAIGHT-SIZED PEOPLE?

Reflection Questions:

Did any of the reading materials in the first section feel relatable/challenging to you? What parts/which ones?

What did that realization feel like for you?

What can you take from that realization? Where can you apply it in the work you are currently doing?

Which of the questions in the internalized fatphobia inventory challenged you to think outside how you usually think?

Did any of the questions in the inventory activity feel new or surprising compared to how you usually see your perceptions of fat and thin/straight-sized people?

Which questions in the internalized fatphobia inventory felt similar to how you feel your own internalized voice sounds when talking about fat people and their choices?

Wrap-up Questions:

Now that you've reached the end of this mini-section, you can take a moment to reflect on the major activity we just did in this section. Write down any feelings that have come up for you in doing the work thus far. How are things feeling? Are you frustrated with the work in this book? The questions? The activities? What feelings are coming up for you?

Feeling Empowered Enough to Ask for Accommodations

Introduction: Something not covered often in literature, social media, and more are the ways that being fat can just be extremely hard physically. So, we're going to talk about some common accommodations you can implement in your life to make being fat while out and about in society easier.

My Accommodation Storytime!

One of the turning points in my own relationship with my body and owning my right to take up space was when I started to advocate for my right to take up room in places where I had previously felt I didn't belong in. This means that in restaurants, I stopped shoving myself into booths. At theaters, I stopped forcing myself into chairs that didn't fit my body just to enjoy a show. Of course, this has meant that I don't go to every event or attraction I want to, and I accept that because my body can't be comfortable or isn't welcome there. I mostly want to be in places where my body is truly and unconditionally welcomed.

I first started advocating for my body in regard to the clothes I wore. This felt like an easier jump than dealing with real human beings who maybe didn't like or want my body in a physical space. So, I started ordering clothes that actually fit my body. This meant, at the time, that I stopped forcing myself to buy "cutesy" clothes that I didn't actually like wearing but fit the mold of what a fat person "should wear". Nope. I opted for t-shirts and sweatshirts—two clothing items that were loose, comfortable, customizable, and graphically appealing! I bought graphic tees from places like TeePublic, and I sized up in sweatshirts so that they were roomy. I searched for underwear made for fat bodies and found companies like Panty Drop and TomboyX and ordered several pairs. I found companies like Big Bud Press and asked my other superfat and infinifat friends where they were finding clothes and shopped there. This allowed me to truly wear clothes I liked and lessened the discomfort of being in clothes that didn't fit or fit uncomfortably while I was out in the world. Wearing clothes that fit you can give you a boost in confidence right off the bat.

Next up in my journey of advocating for myself was the "real world", and I started with restaurants—mainly because that was a situation that occurred rather often. As I said, my main goal was to stop shoving myself into booths where my body was too large or did not fit. And so, my approach to this was to immediately ask when entering a restaurant if I could be sat at a table. And instead of being guided to a booth and having to push back and be adamant about sitting at a table for my own comfort, almost all restaurants have agreed and allowed me to sit at a table. The ones that haven't have been employees who were, for lack of a better word, naive, and when they have watched me try and fit in a booth, they have immediately acquiesced. My advice here is to always stick to your guns. You're paying them to eat there. They are not paying you to be there. And so, it should be up to you what you consider comfortable and acceptable.

Accommodation Activity to Complete:

Let's start out by listing all the places where you feel your body is not given proper respect or the respect it deserves.

* Some examples might be airplanes, restaurants, gyms, doctors' offices, concert venues, etc.

Next, let's list out all the ways you can think of that the particular location/venue could accommodate your body/mobility needs.

* Think of things like larger chairs, more sturdy chairs, weight-neutral commentary, larger-sized clothing, etc.

Now, let's make a plan for how we can either *ask* that place to accommodate us OR find new companies we can invest in/buy from that *will* accommodate us in the way(s) we need.

* For example, I couldn't find comfortable period underwear, but TomboyX goes up to size 6XL and is comfortable and size-inclusive (to a point), but I had to try out a new company in order to find this accommodation.

Lastly, let's make another **"I Commit" Statement** for this week. Let's commit to taking one small step toward accommodating or advocating for ourselves this week—it could be something like speaking up at the doctor's or asking for a table in a restaurant or checking Walmart for weight-inclusive chairs. What will that look like for you this week?

Read This: Advocating for Yourself at the Doctors' Office:

I will not sugar coat this when I say that one of the absolute hardest places to advocate for yourself and your body when you're fat is the doctor's office. It is inherently fatphobic and is, oftentimes, set up to discriminate against you from the get-go. Doctors (even the few doctors who are well-versed in Health at Every Size) have been taught for years to seek out fat patients so that they can "help" them to lose weight, shrink their bodies, and do anything to become thin.

Asher Laramie (they/them/he/him)—a fat doctor in the UK—has created some amazing content from the side of a doctor staunchly against prescribing intentional weight loss. You can find them on Instagram here and some of their really insightful posts to look over here and here.

(🔗 Be sure to follow the QR code at the beginning or find the links at the back of the book as well.)

This reality may feel disheartening. I'd be surprised if it didn't feel that way. But this is why we also learn how to advocate for ourselves, in what ways we can speak up for ourselves, and what is necessary for doctors to know about our bodies—as well as what isn't.

Let's Start with Some Ideas for How to Make Advocating for Yourself Easier:

* Bring along a buddy (they don't have to be a thin/straight-sized body, but you may be taken more "seriously" by your providers if they are) to back you up and also provide moral support.

* Know your rights and preferences based on what will, ultimately, benefit you mentally, emotionally, and physically.

- This can look like refusing to let medical professionals weigh you under the guise of insurance needs (read this post by me here).
- This can also look like choosing to not engage in discussions about prescribed weight loss or weight loss medications. A phrase like, *"That's not an option for me given my medical history."* or *"I have a history of a restrictive eating disorder that would prohibit me from engaging in intentional weight loss."* can be helpful to practice so you remember it when the time comes.

* Read up on materials that are educational as to what weight stigma truly is and how it shows up in your medical care so that, if you encounter it, you will know sooner and can address it, if possible, and stand up for yourself.
    - Some great places to start are the Health at Every Size® Principles on the Association for Size Diversity and Health (ASDAH)'s website.
    - You can also read books like Health at Every Size®: The Surprising Truth About Your Weight by Lindo Bacon (find the book, excerpts, and materials here), BUT there has been much controversy around this book, and some of the content included is outdated material at this point.
        - A note, however, is that the appendix, included here in full, for free, contains letters that you can share with your health providers if you'd like. Some of these documents provide guidelines for providing more sensitive care to fat people.

* Also, make sure to ask around for recommendations on healthcare providers that are HAES-positive, weight-neutral, weight-stigma-educated, etc. Whatever language you feel fits what you're looking for! A great place to ask for support like this is in the Facebook group Caring for Our Fat Bodies, a space for fat people to gather and share advice and compassion, as well as other forms of support. Unfortunately, they've had to make the group private at times, so you may not be able to access it before becoming a member.

And Some Other Links to Further Reading + Articles on this Topic:

* **Comfy Fat** - Advocating For Yourself At The Doctor As A Fat Person Isn't Easy – Here's Where To Start
* **GoodRx Health** - 6 Ways to Advocate for Yourself at the Doctor's Office If You Have a Larger Body
* **Dia&Co** - How to Advocate for Yourself at the Doctor

⭐ **This section has mostly been educational in nature and has contained a hefty info dump. Please feel free to jot down any questions you have in the questions area or in your journal—wherever feels most helpful!**

Read This: Traveling in a Fat Body

Next up! We're discussing one of the things many fat people find the scariest or hardest to do in terms of being fat in "public"—and something I find myself answering questions about often. This tends to be because, in this situation, we are putting ourselves directly in the line of fatphobic remarks and discomfort. You're not alone here! Let's talk about traveling (more specifically, flying) while in a fat body.

First of all, if you're flying/traveling in a fat body any time soon or want to watch a video of me walking you through the best ways to travel in a fat body, go watch the Instagram LIVE I did on @thefriendineverwanted about the topic!

And, if you would rather *read* through the details I discuss in that video (and more) before watching the LIVE, you can start reading on from here!

As I said above, flying, in particular, may feel especially hard or scary when you're in a fat body because, with the exception of luxurious first-class seats, almost all airplane seats are made for thin/straight-sized bodies and not fat bodies. Typical airplane (and train) seats are made for the "average American human", but they forgot to take into account that the true "average American" body comes in a size 14 or larger. 🙄 And so, most of us are left squeezing into too-small-for-our-body seats even when those bodies are small/mid-sized fat bodies and not large fat/superfat/infinifat-sized bodies. It doesn't help that while we are already facing our own internalized fatphobia and shame in these moments, we are often faced by thin/straight-sized people aggressively and outwardly attempting to shame us further about our bodies. Fatphobia is often seen as somewhat acceptable bullying behavior by society, but when it comes to traveling, it's often utilized as a common tactic to verbally berate fat people.

So, in response, when flying or traveling, it's helpful to be the most prepared you can be in order to feel a sense of security while also focusing on things that are within your actual control. Some of these things may include:

* Flying on airlines that accommodate/make room for fat bodies with their policies—like Southwest, in particular for domestic flights
    * Researching things like seat size (SeatGuru.com is great for this), COS (Customer of Size) policies, weight limits, and ADA accommodations
* Reaching out for support around similar experiences from others (see below for Facebook groups to join!)
* Taking safety into consideration by not bringing your own seatbelt extender and, instead, asking for seatbelt extenders from airline personnel
* AND practicing self-talk that reinforces within us the understanding that we are not broken, inferior, or unworthy of the same life choices as our peers in smaller bodies

Every time I've flown since about 2019, I have flown Southwest (unless, for some reason, I absolutely could not), and in those situations, I have utilized their Customer of Size (COS) policy—linked below. In the earlier days, using this policy allowed me to purchase an extra seat at face value to give me more space to sit in and also increase my personal comfort while flying. At first, this experience was scary and a little overwhelming—not to mention expensive! However, in the last year or year and a half, Southwest has changed its policy so every passenger of size is entitled to an extra seat under this policy regardless of if they have purchased it ahead of the flight or not. If you're looking for a walk-through on how to use this policy, this article, "How To Use Southwest's Customer Of Size

Policy in 2023" by Becca Robins[7], does an amazing job of explaining the different steps and has been written for 2023.

Some Things I Specifically Keep in Mind when Flying while Fat and also while Using the Customer of Size Policy at Southwest:

* I always arrive early, even though I have TSA PreCheck now so that I can get my extra seat situated at the check-in counter, have my bags checked if needed, use the restroom in the airport, and wait comfortably at my gate. These are all very important steps and accommodations that I take.

* I pre-board as close to the front of the line as possible so I can have the first or second choice of seats/rows on the plane.

* When boarding, I ask the flight attendant in the front galley for a seatbelt extender right away and wait for them to give it to me. This keeps them from forgetting it and also makes the exchange more private if that feels scary or uncomfortable in any way.

* I usually wait for most people to deplane once we arrive so that I have as much time as I need to get out of the row and into the aisle and then up the jetway.

* I also utilize the airport's wheelchair-pushing service—most importantly on connections and in my arrival city but also, sometimes, in my departing airport on the way home as well. I try to communicate that I need a sturdy or large wheelchair and a strong pusher if they don't automatically pick up on that fact. And I always tip well for the wheelchair pushers who do push me. I tend to tip at least $5/connection or destination service.

✈ **A Note:** Things can become more complicated when traveling for work or brand deals because most companies do not readily assume that their employees will need to purchase two seats. In the event that you're working for a company that requires travel, when that hurdle occurs, it's always best to communicate with your company that you will require purchasing two seats to accommodate your body. They can then decide what they will do in this situation, but all employers or brands I have worked with thus far have always paid for the additional seat when I have requested it. In my opinion, it makes more sense to communicate and ask for what you need and potentially have it granted rather than assume it will not be granted to you and, instead, try to purchase a second seat yourself or force yourself into one seat.

Helpful Websites for Information about Traveling while Fat:

* SeatGuru Seat Map
* Southwest Airlines Customer of Size Policy - find it here
* Southwest's complaint/feedback form - "email" SWA here
* Facebook Groups to Join:
  o Flying while Fat
  o Flying while SuperFat - Generally for people size 28 or 4XL and larger
* Here's my fat-friendly amazon list of products made for fat peeps who just want some awesome stuff made for their bodies!

⭐ **Again, this travel section has mostly been an info dump section with some of my own story thrown in. Please feel free to jot down any realizations or thoughts you have that you want to reflect on here.**

Wrap-up Questions:

Now that you've reached the end of this mini-section, you can take a moment to reflect on the major activity we just did in this section. Write down any feelings that have come up for you in doing the work thus far. How are things feeling? Are you frustrated with the work in this book? The questions? The activities? What feelings are coming up for you?

Part 4

Let's Make It Real

(🔗 Remember to use the QR code at the beginning or find the links at the back of the book when going through.)

Curating or Starting a New, Affirming, Social Media Feed

Introduction: This is going to be the shortest introduction to how to show up on social media if you want to! A note first that showing up on social media can be a great way to hold yourself accountable in this work. What follows will be some suggestions on how to do that, as well as a breakdown of how you can show up, do this work, and create your own community online.

Why Am I Suggesting You Go on Social Media?

If you're not on social media already, then I am baffled by how you found this book. Well... to an extent! If you're here, then you're meant to be here—no matter how you got here.

What I'm talking about is that if you've found this book through social media, that is because, at some point in 2017, I decided to start a new social media account that would let me talk about food and fatness privately, objectionably, and freely. I wanted a place that was mine, outside of the eyes of my friends and family, where I could experiment with recovery, self-love, and body acceptance. But at the time, I just wanted to talk about the trauma I'd experienced in my life without it being tied to me.

This is why I suggest that people in recovery from anti-fat bias—who are working through their own internalized fat bias and learning to stand their ground as a baby fat activist—start their own new + safe social media account...

Creating + Making an Account a Safe Space for You

First and foremost, creating a new account is a safe space for you.

There's no algorithm set to send you diet ads that it's learned you've watched over the past several years. There are no fitspo or thinspo (i.e. "aspirational" pictures of thin, fit, and sometimes emaciated people) accounts you accidentally followed. The Kardashians and their problematic selves aren't set to "post notifications" on this account.

It's a fresh, blank slate.

Don't get me wrong, if you are attached to your account, you don't have to let it go. You can still keep it! I still have my old personal account and check in on it from time to time. But it doesn't serve me in the way it used to anymore. And there are so many diet-y accounts followed on there, too.

But you can curate your account to be safer and better serving for you if you don't want to create a new account!

I'm going to walk you through both options now:

How to Create a New Instagram Account

First, pick a good username. This can be something fun or serious— something related to your journey or the names of your three cats. It doesn't *really* matter. You are always welcome to change it later down the road, but also, now is a good time to reflect on the work you've done so far and, maybe, pick a name or short phrase that's related to that. Also, keep in mind whether you want your account to be anonymous or not.

* Here are the handles of some of my own accounts:
    o @thefriendineverwanted
    o @selflovetoolchest

- @strugsnhugs
- @thatniapatterson

Next up? Actually creating the account. Here are Instagram's Directions on how to do the logistical starting of a new account.

* Once you have a new account set up and you're logged in, here comes the fun part!
* Go ahead and take on any or all of these steps that you feel apply to your current situation:
  - Block your IRL friends if you feel comfortable doing so, and there's a good chance you'll feel much safer posting vulnerable and "real" content this way. Your friends won't know if you did.
  - Choose whether you want to connect your new Instagram account to Facebook so that content is automatically shared to both. I'm GUESSING you may not want that...
    - This means also don't automatically share your account with your Facebook audience when prompted to.
  - Re-follow anyone from your previous account whose content you thoroughly enjoy or that challenges you to think outside the stringent, capitalist box!
  - Follow some great fat joy, fat activism, anti-racism, Queer/trans, and BIPOC accounts! I'm attaching my guide to the best accounts I follow here.
  - Start posting and sharing to your new account.
    - Create graphics in Canva, take pictures wherever you want, and MOST importantly, have fun with it!

- Depending on your personal settings and who you've chosen to block, sharing to hashtags may attract people you know, so just keep that in mind.

✳ And be sure to send me a DM or tag me in your post and let me know that you're part of this journey if it's private or an anonymous account so that I can follow you back!

How to Curate Your Existing Instagram Account

✳ This is how we go about curating an Instagram account that's already up and running and has been affected by ads, the algorithm, and other accounts over the years already! It can feel difficult and arduous, but I promise that it's worth it!

✳ Here are the best steps for going about curating your Instagram feed so that you feel safe and supported online:

  o UNFOLLOW. UNFOLLOW. UNFOLLOW. Get rid of any account that makes you question your worth, feel comparison, or judge yourself.

  o Block your IRL friends or anyone who makes you feel as though you "should" censor yourself online—if you feel comfortable doing so.

  - As a heads up, if they already follow you, they WILL NOT get a notification that you've blocked them, but they may notice that they're not seeing your account, posts, or stories anymore and may reach out to you.

  o If your Instagram is connected to your personal Facebook page, question if you want to keep that connection intact. You may not want that feature on if you're going to be sharing more vulnerable content that highlights what you're going through on a deeper level. It's completely up to you! Just something to keep in mind.

- o Follow as many fat joy, fat activism, anti-racism, Queer/trans, and BIPOC accounts as you can! Fill your feed! I am attaching my guide to the best accounts I follow here.
- o Start posting and sharing content that feels aligned with this evolution of yourself to your account! Create graphics in Canva, take pictures wherever you want, and MOST importantly, have fun with it!

* Now, if you haven't already, be sure to send me a DM or tag me in your post and let me know that you're part of this journey if it's private or an anonymous account so that I can follow you back!

How to Curate a Community on Social Media:

Share your own posts and be authentically you!

* This is the number one thing to do! There's no "right" way to do it either.

* I always recommend that you make your content feel how you actually feel.

- o Are you funny? Add in that!
- o If you're a reader and an intellectual, talk about books that are making a difference in your life right now and connect with others on that level!
- o If you love engaging in nourishing body movement, then connect with some body image movement coaches or the like.

* There's almost always someone out there doing something you like to do, too, and the posts you share may resonate with them deeply and kick off a relationship or bond!

Interact with others and their content.
* This feels like a social media *tactic*, but I promise it's not. The way that Instagram and its algorithm works is that most people don't know other accounts even exist until they come across their notifications feed. So, they won't ever really hear about your account just from likes you leave. You have to take the initiative to speak up and say something, interact, give your opinion or feeling on the topic. Get vulnerable.
* This is how other people know if they want to continue talking to or interacting with you.
* But don't take it personally if they don't respond. Not everyone tends to their comments the way that we should, or someone may have an off day. If you want to talk with someone one-on-one, it's okay to also take the next step and send them a message.
* These *tactics* are how I've made some AMAZING connections over the years with other content creators, activists, brands, and more.

Directly interact with other people through DMs and comments.
* The best way to create relationships with people directly is through DMs. If someone comments on something of yours and you feel like you want to learn more about them, just ask.

* Messaging people can FEEL really scary, but you'll miss every single shot you don't take, and they could end up being a really great supporter, friend, or peer!
* Definitely go for it!

Update your Instagram "Hidden Words" feature.
* First of all, adding words to your "Hidden Words" list can be TRIGGERING because there are some horrible, horrible words and traumatic words, too! Please, please, please, do not look them up! Just copy and paste from the document below directly into your account's "Hidden Words" feature.
* To learn how to add hidden words here's Instagram's instructions on how to do it!
    o You want to especially pay attention to >> **"Manage custom words and phrases"**
    o Here is the link to my hidden words list.

Block trolls and haters.
* This is me giving you full-stop permission to block, report, etc. anyone and everyone you feel is coming at you sideways. If you don't like their vibe, block them. It's okay. I promise. They won't even get a notification. Be gone haters!

Wrap-up Questions:

Now that you've reached the end of this mini-section, you can take a moment to reflect on the major activity we just did in this section. Write down any feelings that have come up for you in doing the work thus far. How are things feeling? Are you frustrated with the work in this book? The questions? The activities? What feelings are coming up for you?

Writing Your Own Fat Liberation Manifesto

Introduction: In this step, you will read about Judy Freespirit and Aldebaran as well as read their original Fat Liberation Manifesto and then go on to create your own Body Liberation Manifesto based on your identities and add in a "call to action" for folks around you to engage with.

A Brief History Lesson:

In 1973, one of the first pioneers of the Fat Liberation Movement, Judy Freespirit, wrote alongside her peer Aldebaran the first Fat Liberation Manifesto. Since then, the tenets of this manifesto have been utilized by fat activists throughout the years to highlight the beliefs central to this social justice movement, as well as to highlight the fact that fat people are just as human and deserving of respect as any other human being or entity. A great first step is to read Judy's manifesto in full here. Take some time to let her words sink in and find resonance within you—or not. But please make note of what does and does not resonate with you, what feels affirming and validating, and what feels alienating or untrue for you.

Activity to Complete Your Own Manifesto:

In this activity, you are going to write your own Body Liberation Manifesto.

* By no means does this have to be shared with anyone—or even ever see the light of day. This is for you and your beliefs and views. If you want to share it, by all means! I would love to see it and hear what went into your creation of it, but if not, I also understand!

Some questions to consider when you're creating your own manifesto:

* Take a look at and look at the structure, wording, and essence of it. How can you apply that to your own manifesto?

* What do Judy and Aldebaran bring to their manifesto that you also want to see in your own manifesto?

* What do Judy and Aldebaran not mention in their manifesto that you wish was mentioned? Can you add that to your own manifesto?

* What other identities that you hold or don't hold do you wish were addressed or highlighted in the manifesto? Can you add them to your manifesto?

* Feel free to jot your manifesto down in your journal or this workbook! You can also create a graphic like I did for the original manifesto to share or not. If you haven't used Canva (a free program) before, it can be a great place to create easy, quick, and simple graphics!

Wrap-up Questions:

Now that you've reached the end of this mini-section, you can take a moment to reflect on the major activity we just did in this section. Write down any feelings that have come up for you in doing the work thus far. How are things feeling? Are you frustrated with the work in this book? The questions? The activities? What feelings are coming up for you?

The Mirror Challenge

Introduction: *This activity is optional because, depending on where you are in your journey, mirror activities can be helpful or can take a toll, become more obsessive than supportive. So, at any point (even right now) that you feel like, "Hey, maybe this isn't for me?" then I say skip right over this step!*

What is the Mirror Challenge?

"The Mirror Challenge" as I've done it is to challenge yourself to see your body, recognize it as it is, and celebrate it for what it does and looks like to you!

When I was doing something more similar to this, it was at a time when I was heavily online, and so I did it more through introspective Instagram photos and posts! This is how it looked like for me at the time:

The point of the challenge is to not be afraid to take pictures. Look at them. Appreciate them. Appreciate YOU IN them. Please note that this is not meant to be a form of "body checking" but, instead, a chance for you to become more comfortable with your body and how it shows up in the world.

For me, I learned that my body wasn't "disgusting" or "inferior" like I had always understood it to be. No, it was just a body—a neutral piece of the world's matter and makeup. How my body presented was not a "do or die" sentence. It just was (is).

How To Do the Mirror Challenge?

Recurring for several days, a week, two weeks, a month, etc.—whatever feels doable and comfortable for you—you take a photo of yourself or take some time in front of the mirror.

If you're taking photos, maybe jot down some thoughts and post them to social media. Or add them to an album in your phone's photo album. Just find a place where you can keep your thoughts and/or feelings about your body and yourself alongside the corresponding photo.

A great way to do this is also posting it to "Close Friends" on Instagram (you don't even have to add anyone to close friends!).

If you're taking time in front of the mirror instead, you can chat with yourself in the mirror, take out your journal, and write about your experience. Maybe make a note of what happened that day that may have triggered any particular feelings or experiences for you prior to standing there.

Mirror Challenge Tracker

You can find the official tracker in a couple pages, or you can simply make notes when you do the challenge.

Some questions to ask yourself are:

* *What did you come across—both emotionally and physically?*

* *Which option did you choose (social or mirror)?*

* *Did you do it alone?*

* *Did you delete any of the photos you took?*

* *How did you decide which days you would show up for the challenge?*

* *Did you share your experience with anyone else? What did they say?*

Mirror Activity
TRACKER

Wrap-up Questions:

Now that you've reached the end of this mini-section, you can take a moment to reflect on the major activity we just did in this section. Write down any feelings that have come up for you in doing the work thus far. How are things feeling? Are you frustrated with the work in this book? The questions? The activities? What feelings are coming up for you? What did you learn, in particular, from the Mirror Challenge?

Showing Up for Yourself in the "Real World"

Introduction: Showing up for ourselves in the "real world" can be super hard. And we need to talk about how this might look, what this might feel like, and/or the ways that you can implement the work we're doing here outside of this workbook!

A Note About this Work:

A post that @heysharonmaxwell, a friend of mine, shared recently on social media left a deep imprint on my heart. And that was that regardless of the work we do for ourselves and on ourselves, there will still be hostility and violence toward marginalized people in the world—marginalized people will have to be in and experience these events. I don't say this to say that there's no hope or that the world can't get better. I truly believe it can. BUT while it's baking into a better world, I want to give you all the tools I can to make you and your resolution as strong as possible. I want you to be able to live a fulfilling life, even when faced with struggles or hostility.

Ways that We can Show Up for Ourselves in the World:

These are some ideas. Maybe they won't all "fit" for you. Maybe they will! You are also welcome to drum up some of your own ideas and add to this list!

Speaking Up for Yourself in Situations of Anti-Fatness

* This is meant along the lines of speaking up when someone displays anti-fat bias.
    o If that means at the doctor's office, okay.

- o   If that means at family dinners, okay.
- o   If that means when talking to your kiddo's little league coach, okay.
* Whatever this looks like in your world, take the step to speak up about it and push back against that anti-fatness that's being portrayed that not only do you feel more rooted in your truth but they feel less rooted in their prejudice.
* Please note that the outcome of this is often doing the educational work for others that they have chosen not to do themselves yet—or at all. You may end up teaching others about weight stigma or anti-fat bias. When taking this approach, you have to be aware of this and your own emotional capacity to do so or not do so.

Engage in Dialogue and/or Discussion around Anti-Fat Bias and Educate Others about What You Know

* This could be in various settings. When writing this, I was picturing in a community group or a support group. This could be a community eating disorder recovery group where you bring up the fact that fat people are discriminated against at such a high rate that it specifically affects your recovery from your eating disorder.
* You can also seek out intergroup dialogue spaces to have these conversations in. These may not be safe or protected spaces, and so you have to take that into consideration, but sitting down with other marginalized people to discuss systemic oppression, anti-racism work, feminism, and fat activism may be helpful for you!

* You are also more than welcome to start your own group and invite others to join in! Both an online or in-person format could be options here.

Putting the Activities and Actions We Have Covered During this Book into Action

* This can mean standing up for yourself when you visit public places.
* Asking for accommodations like:
  - Making sure you're given a comfortable seat in restaurants,
  - Wearing comfortable clothing when you want to,
  - Having accessible tools and seating at home and at friends' houses;
  - Just to list a few!
* What else would you add to this list?

A BIG ONE! Ask for Help or Support When You Need it

* This doesn't have to be physical support. It can be emotional support, too—or relationship support.
* You are allowed to find and have the support you need in your life. I guarantee you that this is something that is made for you and totally okay to seek out!

Share this Book with Other Fat and Marginalized People Who Might Benefit from it

* Sharing is almost always caring!
* Share this book with other people in your life who you feel would or could benefit from digging into their own anti-fat bias and exploring

what life looks like on the other side of direct struggle—where you can take up the space you deserve to take up in the world. If you know someone who is on this journey or doing this work, please do not hesitate to share this with them!

Wrap-up Questions:

Now that you've reached the end of this mini-section, you can take a moment to reflect on the major activity we just did in this section. Write down any feelings that have come up for you in doing the work thus far. How are things feeling? Are you frustrated with the work in this book? The questions? The activities? What feelings are coming up for you?

Part 5

You Did It!

(🔗 Remember to use the QR code at the beginning or find the links at the back of the book when going through.)

What You "Should" Know Now

Where "Should" You Be on Your Journey Now?

I use the "should" term very loosely here because, as you may have gathered by now, "should" can be a word easily weaponized against ourselves to tell us to "do better" and "be better" when, really and truly, we are doing just fine and are more than enough. Ideally, at this point in the book, you will know the steps to advocate for yourself in various situations of anti-fatness. You will, hopefully, know some ways to actively question your own internalized anti-fat bias and take steps to do so in situations where it feels triggered. I hope you have confronted (or begun to confront) your personal fears of becoming fatter and/or gaining weight, and in situations where that feels tangible, you are able to reframe some or all of those thoughts that are negative or unserving. Now, you may be able to take care of yourself adequately in situations where you face anti-fat bias, or at least have some responses that you can lean on to respond to that situation, or be able to walk away. And, in the event that anything happens negatively or violently toward you, I hope you have begun to form a community you can lean on in these times for direct care and support.

This may sound like A LOT that you have learned in this book! But keep in mind, not one of these things has to be perfect or "completed". Our own journeys to reclaiming our bodies and reframing our internalized prejudice are ever-ongoing. My main goal is to set you up for success and push you (gently) out of the nest into the greater world beyond you with the tools, skills, and outlook to disrupt and heal.

Questions I Have for You Now

Do you feel as though you have made forward progress with your body acceptance journey, internalized anti-fat bias, and/or body image struggles through the world with this book?

If so, in what ways have you made forward progress? What does that look like/feel like for you now?

If not, in what ways do you feel you have remained stuck where you started, or even backtracked, in your progress? What does that look like/feel like for you now?

How have you felt supported throughout this book? In what ways could you find similar support outside of this book now that it is coming to an end? Will you seek out that support?

Can you think of anyone around you who may need similar support as you have gotten through this book? Can you think of a way to get this book in their hands?

Tell Me Your Thoughts Activity:

If you wouldn't mind, I'd love to hear from you and what your thoughts have been during and at the end of this book! If you'd be kind enough to reach out to me via email at hello@niapatterson.com or on Insta @thefriendineverwanted with an honest testimonial of the book and your experience reading it, I would GREATLY appreciate it!

Wrap-up Thoughts:

You've reached the end! This is your LAST wrap-up! Woot, woot! So, do me [and yourself] a favor and jot down some thoughts about the journey you've gone through in this book. Please go ahead and take a moment to reflect on the various parts, activities, and questions sprinkled throughout. Write down any feelings that have come up for you in doing this *hard* work. How are things feeling now? What's coming up for you?

Resources

Cited Sources:

[6] Doyle, Glennon. https://momastery.com/blog/about-glennon/.

[3] Duckworth, S. (2020). *The Wheel of Power/Privilege* [Photograph]. Instagram.
   https://www.instagram.com/p/CEFiUShhpUT/?hl=en

[5] Elrod, Hal. 2012. *The Miracle Morning: The Not-So-Obvious Secret Guaranteed to Transform Your Life (Before 8 AM)*. 1st ed. Hal Elrod.

[1] Gordon, A. (2020, July 22). *Having a Better Body Image Won't End Body-Based Oppression*. Self. Retrieved November 5, 2023, from
   https://www.self.com/story/body-neutrality

[4] "Neuroplasticity and How Rewiring Is Important to Recovery." SIDE BY SIDE NUTRITION. May 22, 2019.
   https://sidebysidenutrition.com/blog/2019/5/21/neuroplasticity-and-how-rewiring-is-important-to-recovery.

[2] Olsson, Jona. "Cage of Oppression." Cultural Bridges to Justice. Cultural Bridges to Justice, Accessed October 31, 2023.
   https://culturalbridgestojustice.org/cage-of-oppression/.

[7] Robins, Becca. "How To Use Southwest's Customer Of Size Policy in 2023." This Crazy Adventure Called Life. July 20, 2023.
   https://thiscrazyadventurecalledlife.com/guide-southwest-customer-of-size/.

Linked Content from Book:

PART 1
Social Post Suggestions:
* [Body Image is Not the Same As...](https://www.instagram.com/p/Csl86BKua0m/) - https://www.instagram.com/p/Csl86BKua0m/
* [What Body Image Actually Is...](https://www.instagram.com/p/CtC7-oQve6d/) - https://www.instagram.com/p/CtC7-oQve6d/
* [Body Neutrality](https://www.instagram.com/p/CtHgkdAOOzQ/) - https://www.instagram.com/p/CtHgkdAOOzQ/
* [Weight Loss is Not the Solution](https://www.instagram.com/p/CLUCw2lFfoi/) - https://www.instagram.com/p/CLUCw2lFfoi/
* [Why "Fat" Became a Bad Word](https://www.instagram.com/p/CMr9a7_FX79/) - https://www.instagram.com/p/CMr9a7_FX79/
* [Black + Brown Bodies and Eating Disorders](https://www.instagram.com/p/B9EiuselAdu/) - https://www.instagram.com/p/B9EiuselAdu/
* [Fat is an Access Issue](https://www.instagram.com/p/B2cUpwuFpHo/) - https://www.instagram.com/p/B2cUpwuFpHo/

Articles: (Trigger Warning: Ob*sity slur may be used)
* [Weight Discrimination: A Socially Acceptable Injustice By Rebecca Puhl](https://www.obesityaction.org/resources/weight-discrimination-a-socially-acceptable-injustice/) - https://www.obesityaction.org/resources/weight-discrimination-a-socially-acceptable-injustice/
* [Yes, You Can Still Be Fired for Being Fat By Josh Eidelson](https://www.bloomberg.com/news/features/2022-03-15/weight-discrimination-remains-legal-in-most-of-the-u-s) - https://www.bloomberg.com/news/features/2022-03-15/weight-discrimination-remains-legal-in-most-of-the-u-s
* [Fat Is Not the Problem—Fat Stigma Is By Lindo Bacon, Amee Severson](https://blogs.scientificamerican.com/observations/fat-is-not-the-problem-fat-stigma-is/) - https://blogs.scientificamerican.com/observations/fat-is-not-the-problem-fat-stigma-is/

TV Shows/Movies:
* [Dietland](https://www.imdb.com/title/tt5869202/) - https://www.imdb.com/title/tt5869202/
* [Shrill](https://www.imdb.com/title/tt8962130/) - https://www.imdb.com/title/tt8962130/
* [Survival of the Thickest](https://www.imdb.com/title/tt17361756/) - https://www.imdb.com/title/tt17361756/
* [Fattitude](https://www.imdb.com/title/tt3916628/) - https://www.imdb.com/title/tt3916628/
* [Your Fat Friend](https://www.imdb.com/title/tt27550024/) - https://www.imdb.com/title/tt27550024/

Additional Resources:
* Diagram: The ["Cage of Oppression"](https://culturalbridgestojustice.org/cage-of-oppression/) - https://culturalbridgestojustice.org/cage-of-oppression/

* Definition of "Lookism" - https://www.oxfordreference.com/display/10.1093/oi/authority.20110803100114487

PART 2

Articles:

* Article: The Antidote to ADHD Fatigue and Exhaustion? Stacking Habits (and Spoons) - https://www.additudemag.com/fatigue-adhd-spoon-theory-habit-stacking/
* Article: Neuroplasticity and How Rewiring is Important to Recovery - https://sidebysidenutrition.com/blog/2019/5/21/neuroplasticity-and-how-rewiring-is-important-to-recovery

PART 3

Social Posts Mentioned:

* Instagram Post: About Being Neutral Toward Your Body - https://www.instagram.com/p/CtHgkdAOOzQ/
* Instagram Account: Asher Larmie - https://www.instagram.com/thefatdoctor/
  * Instagram Post by Asher Larmie - https://www.instagram.com/p/CuRh7QjogDI/
  * Instagram Post by Asher Larmie - https://www.instagram.com/p/CtrFEeSoyRQ/
* Instagram Post by Nia Patterson - https://www.instagram.com/p/CMhWggqpONf
* Instagram LIVE: Re: Flying While Fat - https://www.instagram.com/p/Cs4rudNJFU5/

Websites Mentioned:

* Website: My Fat-Friendly Amazon Affiliate List - https://amzn.to/3QpQuqX
* Clothing Website: Teepublic - https://www.teepublic.com/
* Clothing Website: Panty Drop - https://www.pantydrop.me/
* Clothing Website: TomboyX - https://tomboyx.com/
* Clothing Website: Big Bud Press - https://bigbudpress.com/

- ✳ Health at Every Size® Principles - https://asdah.org/health-at-every-size-haes-approach/
- ✳ Association for Size Diversity and Health (ASDAH) - https://www.asdah.org/
- ✳ Health at Every Size®: The Surprising Truth About Your Weight by Lindo Bacon - https://amzn.to/3FLA3P1
  - o Health at Every Size: Excerpts and Downloads - https://lindobacon.com/health-at-every-size-book/haes-excerpts-and-downloads/
  - o Health at Every Size Appendix - https://lindabacon.org/health-at-every-size-book/haes-excerpts-and-downloads/
- ✳ Website: SeatGuru - https://www.seatguru.com/
  - o SeatGuru Seat Map - https://www.seatguru.com/findseatmap/findseatmap.php
- ✳ Website: Southwest Airlines Customer of Size Policy - https://www.southwest.com/help/booking/extra-seat-policy
- ✳ Website: Southwest's complaint/feedback form - https://support.southwest.com/email-us/s/

Facebook Groups to Check Out and/or Join:
- ✳ Flying while Fat - https://www.facebook.com/groups/flyingwhilefat/
- ✳ Flying while SuperFat - Generally for people size 28 or 4XL and larger - https://www.facebook.com/groups/926214367418144/
- ✳ Caring for Our Fat Bodies - https://www.facebook.com/groups/302128423576431/

Articles Mentioned:
- ✳ Article: How To Use Southwest's Customer Of Size Policy in 2023 by Becca Robins - https://thiscrazyadventurecalledlife.com/guide-southwest-customer-of-size/

Additional Recommended Articles:

* Comfy Fat - Advocating For Yourself At The Doctor As A Fat Person Isn't Easy – Here's Where To Start - https://comfyfat.com/2019/06/01/advocating-for-yourself-at-the-doctor/
* GoodRx Health - 6 Ways to Advocate for Yourself at the Doctor's Office If You Have a Larger Body - https://www.goodrx.com/health-topic/weight/how-to-advocate-at-doctor
* Dia&Co - How to Advocate for Yourself at the Doctor - https://www.dia.com/blog/wellness/how-to-advocate-for-yourself-at-the-doctor/
* 12 Good Fatty Archetypes - https://stacybias.net/2014/06/12-good-fatty-archetypes/

PART 4

Social Accounts Mentioned:

* @thefriendineverwanted - https://www.instagram.com/thefriendineverwanted/
* @selflovetoolchest - https://www.instagram.com/selflovetoolchest/
* @strugsnhugs - https://www.instagram.com/strugsnhugs/
* @thatniapatterson - https://www.instagram.com/thatniapatterson/
* Some of The Best Accounts I Follow - https://drive.google.com/file/d/1KS9vxzOvp5sOwzdz_HN1e4XpVAfWQKU1/view
* @HeySharonMaxwell's Post - https://www.instagram.com/reel/Cuvrn8Gx_MN/

Articles Mentioned:

* Article: How to Start a New Instagram Account - https://help.instagram.com/155940534568753
* Article: How to Add Hidden Words to Your Account - https://help.instagram.com/700284123459336?helpref=faq_content
    o My Hidden Words List - https://docs.google.com/document/d/1Awkac0kh6xT_P6V0uXq-DHJWHehY4Z7SNRhtnjGtL4g/view

Websites Mentioned:

* Website: [Fat Liberation Manifesto by Judy Freespirit and Aldebaran](#) - https://laurietobyedison.com/body-impolitic-blog/tag/fat-liberation-manifesto/
* Website: ["The Fategories"](#) by [Fluffy Kitten Party](#) - https://fluffykittenparty.com/2021/06/01/fategories-understanding-smallfat-fragility-the-fat-spectrum/
* Website: [The History of the Word 'Superfat'](#) - https://cherrymax.medium.com/community-origins-of-the-term-superfat-9e98e1b0f201
* Website: [Ash Fat Lip](#) - [Creator of the Word 'Infinifat'](#) - http://thefatlip.com/2016/12/20/beyond-superfat-rethinking-the-farthest-end-of-the-fat-spectrum/

Tools/Applications Mentioned:

* Website/Tool: [Canva](#) - https://www.canva.com/
* Application:
  o Instagram ([Apple Store](#)) - https://apps.apple.com/us/app/instagram/id389801252
  o Instagram ([Google Play](#)) - https://play.google.com/store/apps/details?id=com.instagram.android&hl=en_IN
  o Instagram ([Microsoft](#)) - https://apps.microsoft.com/detail/9NBLGGH5L9XT?hl=en-fj&gl=FJ

Glossary

Glossary

Target Identity groups are those social identity groups that are positioned as targeted by oppression, to be disenfranchised, subordinated, exploited, and/or otherwise harmed.

Agent Identity groups are those social identity groups that are positioned to be afforded agency, advantaged, dominant, and hold unearned privilege in society.

Body Checking is the compulsive monitoring of your body's shape or weight. It usually involves frequent behaviors like weighing yourself, scrutinizing your body parts in the mirror, or even seeking reassurance about potential changes in physical appearance from others. These habits often include comparing your body to pictures of your past self or other people and judging your body size based on clothing fit. This obsessive pattern is often indicative of underlying body image issues or a disordered relationship between food and body.

An **Eating Disorder** is a range of psychological conditions that cause unhealthy eating habits to develop. They might start with an obsession with food, body weight, or body shape. In severe cases, eating disorders can cause serious health consequences and may even result in death if left untreated. In fact, eating disorders are among the deadliest mental illnesses, second to opioid overdose. People with eating disorders can have a variety of symptoms. Common symptoms include severe restriction of food, food binges, and purging behaviors like vomiting or overexercising. Although eating disorders can affect people of any gender at any life stage, they're increasingly common in men and gender-nonconforming people. These populations often seek treatment at lower rates or may not report their eating disorder symptoms at all.

Disordered Eating are food- and diet-related behaviors that don't meet diagnostic criteria for recognized eating disorders (EDs) but may still negatively affect someone's physical, mental, or emotional health. This can be especially true for people who don't match the stereotypes surrounding eating disorders, such as People of Color, men, and people at higher body weights.

Body-Based Oppression is about how the world around us *treats* our bodies. So, for example, a fat, disabled person might not have issues with how they see their own body but may struggle with a lack of acceptance from those around them and in the environments they're in. Conversely, a thin, white, able-bodied person may struggle mightily with an eating disorder but not have to contend with the same kind of street harassment, discrimination, or access issues that many of us whose bodies are marked by differences do.

Various Sizes of Fat Bodies - Information here is pulled from "The Fategories" by Linda at FluffyKittenParty. Here are some great graphics/diagrams of the Fategories:

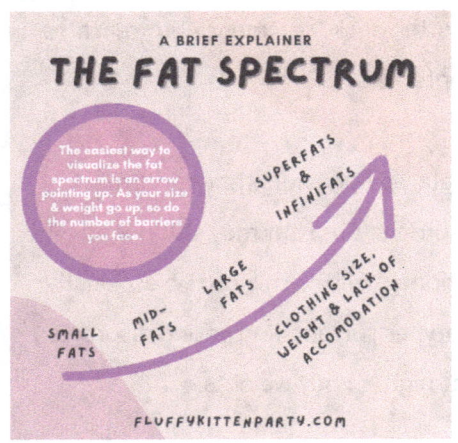

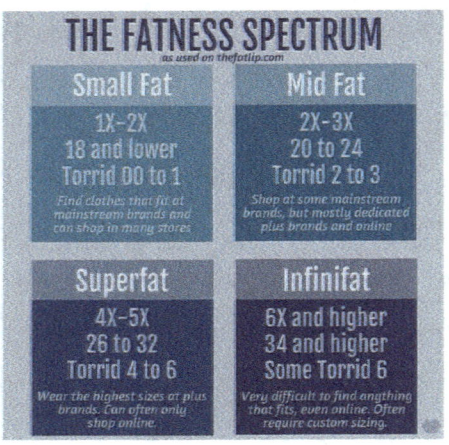

Straight-Size: A "straight-size" person is, quite simply, someone who is not fat. They do not require plus-size clothing, and their body weight is not generally a barrier for them in their daily lives.

Small Fat: Below a US women's 18, or in the 1x-2x range. A "small fat" is someone on the smallest end of the fat spectrum. Think "entry level" fat. When it comes to plus-size clothing, they are included in the size ranges of all plus-size retailers, as well as many straight-size clothes. A person who is in the small fat range may experience some degree of size oppression (such as doctors voicing concern about their weight or comments from friends, family, or people in general), but they are able to access public spaces and are, generally, not shut out of many areas of life solely due to their weight.

Mid-Fat: Between a US women's 20-24 or 26, or 2x-3x. "Mid-fat" people are the next step up the fat spectrum. Mid-fats are typically relegated to plus-size retailers and rarely included in straight-size retailers' extended sizes. At this stage, brick-and-mortar options for clothing tend to dry up, as most options are online-only. Institutional sizeism comes into play much more strongly with mid-fats than small fats. People in the "mid-fat" range are likely to experience discrimination or stigma in healthcare, at work, in relationships, and the world at large. They may have trouble fitting into certain seats or accessing certain spaces. However, they are still accommodated to some degree, in comparison to those who are on the larger end of the spectrum.

Large Fat: US women's 26-32, or 4x-5x. Definitions of "large fat" can vary, but the term usually refers to people in between the "mid-fat" and "super fat" categories. This term is, sometimes, used interchangeably with "Lane Bryant Fat", a term coined by writer Roxane Gay. People who consider themselves "large fat" are on the larger side of the middle of the fatness spectrum, which is a bit of a confusing sentence—sorry about that.

Superfat: Women's size 26 and up; may have an upper limit or not, depending on who is using this label and how they choose to employ it. Read the history of the word here. You can, generally, always assume that when someone refers to themselves as "super fat", they mean they are on the larger end of the size spectrum. People in this range experience a lack of access due to their weight on a regular, daily basis. They experience discrimination in healthcare, the workplace, public spaces, and are excluded from many areas of public life. People who identify as superfat are either at the upper end of most plus-size retailers or may even be sized out of most plus-size retailers. They generally have no brick-and-mortar clothing stores that serve them.

Infinifat: Women's US size 32-34 and above, or may be used as a variant of super fat. The term "infinifat" was created by Ash of The Fat Lip. "Infinifat" people face significant barriers due to institutionalized sizeism on a daily basis. As defined by the graphic Ash made (which is widely circulated), infinifat refers to anyone who is a size 34 or above and/or size 6x. Infinifats are so underserved that many may not know their actual clothing size because plus-size retailers do not include them at all. They may have to have clothing made custom. People in this size range are excluded from participating in many areas of public life, face intense discrimination and mistreatment in healthcare, and are the most underserved of all members of the fat community.

Acknowledgements

First, I absolutely, positively must thank my family. In particular, Gram, Glendora, GP. Without your support and steadfast presence in my life throughout all thirty-one years to this point, I would not be here.

My closest friends (and practically family), Ayesha, Amee, Olivia, Lara, and Ashley, each of you have shown up for me in so many ways that have allowed me to be the creative human being that I am, and I thank you for that.

Jenesis, thank you for coaching me to create Breaking Body Barriers and this book too.

This book is about recovery, it's about mental health, and body image, and body liberation. There are people, hundreds, thousands, who have impacted my life throughout the eating disorder recovery and body liberation communities on social media and the real-world spaces made for all bodies to exist. Without knowing it maybe, you have left an impact on my life.

I also must thank the people along this journey that are no longer by my side. Without your presence in my life, I wouldn't have learned how important my recovery was and is to me. You taught me about stubbornness, showing up for myself, friendship, and so much more.

I ABSOLUTELY must thank the Wednesday night support group crew in Camarillo, CA. You all were my toe dip into recovery, and you sustained that in me for years. You kept my head above water.

Kelly, Danielle, Monica, Michelle, Leslie, Erin, Kim - each of you have shown up to provide me treatment and care throughout my time in recovery.

To my therapist, Liz. I am so lucky I have been your client since 2020. Thank you for being vocal about your beliefs, your strengths, your thoughts, your pet peeves, and yourself. You taught me that despite all the broccoli and [metaphorical] dead puppies shoved behind the cardboard wall; I too can be an amazing human. I am so much stronger, better, and wiser for knowing you.

And to the woman who didn't let me cry it out at night and let me know every day that I was her "favorite kid in all the world," thank you Bibi, for letting me know I will always belong.

Level 10 Life

WORKSHEET

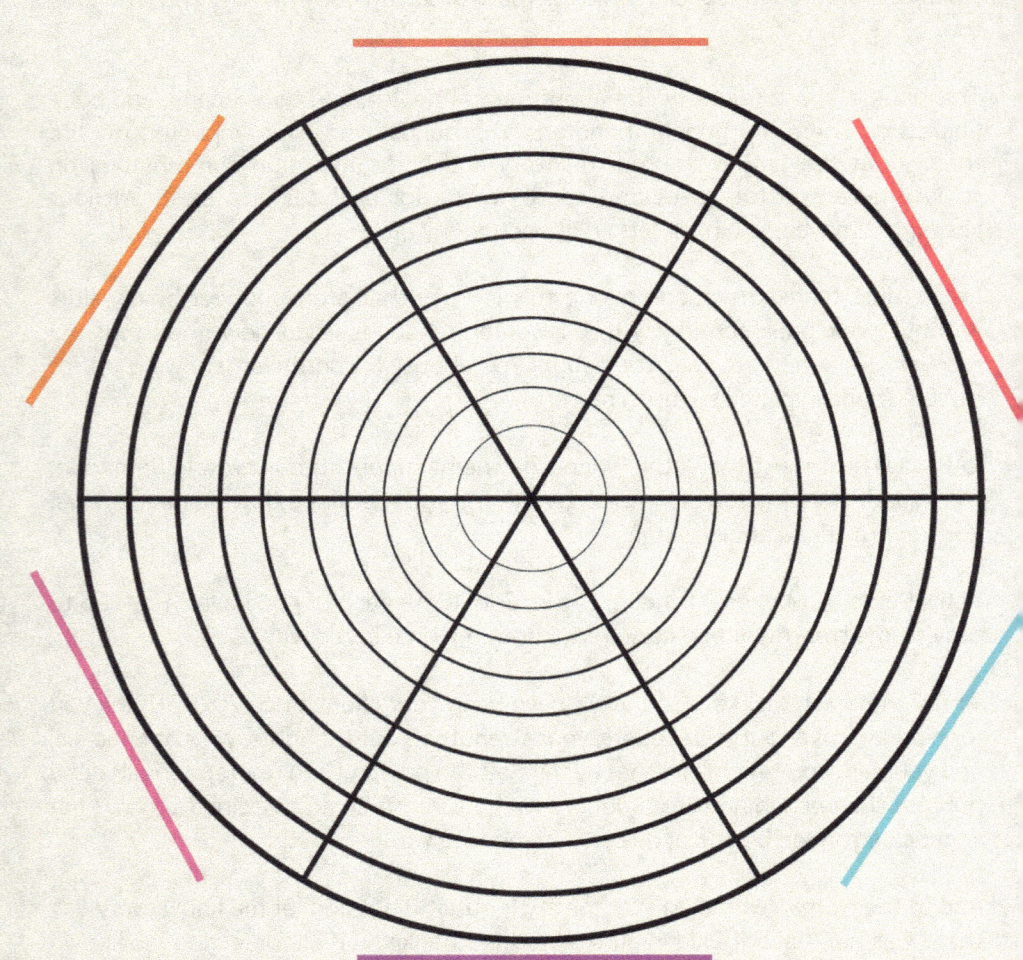

Level 10 Life

WORKSHEET